Math Misconceptions

PreK–Grade 5

From Misunderstanding to Deep Understanding

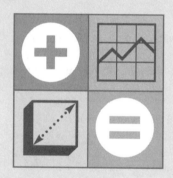

Honi J. Bamberger

Christine Oberdorf

Karren Schultz-Ferrell

HEINEMANN ✹ Portsmouth, NH

HEINEMANN
361 Hanover Street
Portsmouth, NH 03801–3912
www.heinemann.com

Offices and agents throughout the world

Library of Congress Cataloging-in-Publication Data
Bamberger, Honi Joyce.
  Math misconceptions : preK–grade 5 : from misunderstanding to deep understanding / Honi J. Bamberger, Christine Oberdorf, Karren Schultz-Ferrell.
      p. cm.
  Includes bibliographical references and index.
  ISBN-13: 978-0-325-02613-8
  ISBN-10: 0-325-02613-0
  1. Mathematics—Study and teaching (Preschool)—United States. 2. Mathematics—Study and teaching (Primary)—United States. 3. Mathematics—Study and teaching (Elementary)—United States. I. Oberdorf, Christine. II. Schultz-Ferrell, Karren. III. Title.
    QA135.6.B366 2010
    372.7—dc22   2010016301

EDITOR: *Victoria Merecki*
PRODUCTION: *Sonja S. Chapman & Elizabeth Valway*
COVER DESIGN: *Night & Day Design*
INTERIOR DESIGN: *Jenny Jensen Greenleaf*
COMPOSITION: *Publishers' Design and Production Services, Inc.*
MANUFACTURING: *Steve Bernier*

Printed in the United States of America on acid-free paper
14 13 12 11 10 VP 1 2 3 4 5

Contents

Foreword

STEVEN LEINWAND

Nearly all of our students make mathematical mistakes—often perfectly logical mistakes based on common misunderstandings. Nearly all of our students are sometimes confused—often in very understandable ways that emerge from their efforts to make sense of new material. Effective teachers have always understood that mistakes and confusion are powerful learning opportunities. Moreover, they understand that one of their critical roles is to anticipate these misconceptions in their lesson planning and to have at their disposal an array of strategies to address common misunderstandings *before* they expand, solidify, and undermine confidence. And when, despite our best intentions, misconceptions present themselves, effective teachers are ready with an array of approaches that address these misconceptions head-on before they fester into serious disability.

Some of these common misconceptions are rather familiar:

- $\frac{3}{8} + \frac{2}{8} = \frac{5}{16}$ because "you add the tops and add the bottoms"

- $.23 > .4$ because $23 > 4$

- if $14 = \_\_\_ + 7$, then 21 goes in the blank because $14 + 7 = 21$

- circles can't have areas of *square* inches or *square* centimeters

- squares are not rectangles because "they have four equal sides"

- $\frac{1}{2} < \frac{1}{3}$ because $2 < 3$

- the probability of spinning a 1 on the spinner shown is $\frac{1}{3}$ because there are three numbers or $\frac{1}{5}$ because there are five segments

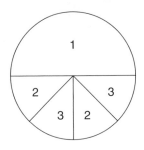

Others types of misconceptions are less familiar:

- decimals get smaller as they grow longer to the right of the decimal point

- graph scale errors

- telling time

- measurement conversion errors

- graphing points in the coordinate plane

- confusing expected vs. experimental results

- three-dimensional spatial visualization

Too often, however, we tend to focus overwhelmingly in mathematics classrooms on right answers and correct processes to get these right answers. Too often, wrong answers are met with a simple, but not very helpful, "no" or "wrong" or a big red X, instead of being probed for the source of the error or underpinning of the misconception. And while some errors are certainly careless or based on a lack of fundamental knowledge (for example, confusing area and perimeter), many student errors arise from one or more misconceptions—misconceptions that arise so often they can almost be catalogued. Consider the perfectly understandable direction to "add a zero" when multiplying by ten being interpreted by students as "adding nothing" to the number! No wonder they are so confused when we magically change 34 to 340, explaining that "we added a zero." In other words, so often, students aren't "wrong" so much as they don't "get it" or they're overgeneralizing, or they're misled by words or rules that don't apply.

In this wonderfully insightful book, Honi, Christine, and Karren not only describe a vast array of perfectly understandable mathematical misconceptions that students have across the elementary curriculum, they also provide a brief research basis that gives a context for these misconceptions. But most helpfully, they provide an array of practical instructional strategies and activities for helping remediate and undo the misconceptions. The classroom vignettes they describe will ring true to everyone who has tried to teach mathematics to young, and not-so-young, children. Experienced teachers will smile and recall that it was Kyle or Alicia who "used to do that." New teachers will recognize that the incorrect explanation that Sarah provided yesterday is really pretty typical among students learning mathematics.

Through the realistic, and frighteningly familiar, classroom vignettes that are provided for each mathematical topic, teachers will discover the power of classroom norms in which children are expected to explain their thinking as a fundamental classroom practice for exploring students' understanding and identifying possible misunderstanding. The vignettes realistically capture both teacher questioning and student thinking—on-target and not as on-target—in ways that transport the reader into the world of real students in real classrooms wrestling with important mathematical ideas.

But the real power of this book lies in the example-laden Ideas for Instruction that follow the vignettes and accompany each of the topics that are explored. Here one finds ideas for activities that provide opportunities for student to represent, construct, visualize, draw, connect, explain, and describe. In other words, the key message is that we can prevent or minimize many common misconceptions and effectively address those that still emerge when our instruction consistently probes students' understandings and provides opportunities for students to show and explain their reasoning. That's the type of mathematics instruction every student deserves and that this book advocates and describes.

So while misconceptions serve as the organizing spine of this book, the subtext is providing effective, high-quality mathematics instruction at all times. Of course it is essential that teachers recognize and anticipate misconceptions and even understand the research findings that help to explain these misunderstandings, but it is the instructional tasks, the ongoing classroom discourse, and the embedded formative assessment—all components of good instruction and the activities that comprise the "Ideas for Instruction"—that make the real difference in student learning of mathematics.

Acknowledgments

Writing books takes a discipline that goes above and beyond the call of duty, especially as we've juggled full-time jobs. We'd like to thank all of the editors at Heinemann whose assistance and patience allowed us to take the time we needed to "get it right." We also appreciate the sacrifices that our families (husbands, children, and even grandchildren) have made as we've taken time away from them to complete these books. Thank you, too, to Govans Elementary and to Oak View Elementary for allowing us to photograph children and activities for the books and for supporting us as we worked on them. Finally, a special thanks to the educators who inspire us and remind us to continue to learn as much as we can so we can inspire them.

Introduction

Making sense is at the heart of mathematics and so it must also be at the heart of the mathematics we do with young children.

—KATHY RICHARDSON

C hildren enter prekindergarten filled with ideas about numbers, shapes, measuring tools, time, and money. They formulate these ideas through their visual and auditory experiences—the expressions they hear adults say and the things they see on television, computer screens, in children's literature, and all around them. It's no wonder that some children develop very interesting and perhaps incorrect ideas about mathematical concepts.

"I can count to a million," a child says as he works with classmates at a number center. "I can count to a million zillion," responds his friend, naming an even bigger number.

Once prekindergartners have learned to identify all ten digits in the numeration system, they often try to make sense of time on a digital clock. "It's two dot dot one four," a four-year-old might say. While they may have no idea what this means, they are making sense of what they've heard about numerals and shapes. And, third through fifth graders seem to repeat what they hear all the time from adults who mispronounce numerals. It's not uncommon to hear a student read the numeral "2010" as two thousand and ten, even though it should be read as two thousand ten. Often what they hear is what they say.

How can we, as early childhood and elementary educators, connect the informal knowledge that students bring to our classrooms with the mathematics program adopted by our school system? Just as important, how do we ensure that the mathematics we are introducing and reinforcing is accurate and appropriate and will not need to be retaught or reexplained in later school years?

▣ What We See in Classrooms

In our travels to classrooms across the country, we see teachers who *care* about their students. Men and women who decide to work with prekindergarten through fifth-grade students do so because they enjoy working with young children and want to help them develop a strong foundation for learning. By and large, these educators are nurturing and supportive and have students' best interests in mind. They want their students to enjoy learning and end the academic year with all the skills and concepts necessary for continued success.

But these positive characteristics can sometimes lead teachers to unwittingly encourage serious error patterns, misconceptions, and overgeneralizations on the part of young learners. For example, one of the big ideas developed in a typical first-grade classroom is making sense of addition and subtraction concepts and learning strategies to obtain basic fact fluency. It is not unusual to hear a classroom teacher say, "Now, remember boys and girls, we always subtract the smaller number from the larger number." Students see a story problem such as *Maria has 6 candies. She gives her friend, Juan, 2 of her candies. How many candies does Maria have now?*, look at the "2" and the "6," think which is the lesser, and subtract the lesser number from the greater number, giving them the correct difference.

The problem is, young children do not always differentiate between numeral, number, and digit. At the end of first grade or at the beginning of second grade, when they begin to use two-digit numbers, students see 23 – 4, remember what the teacher has said, take the smaller *digit* away from the greater *digit*, and end up with a difference of *21*.

Does this error occur only because of what some teachers have said? Of course not. There are many other reasons students subtract in this manner. But in "helping" students make sense of subtraction with seemingly innocent supports, some teachers inadvertently create more problems. And it isn't true that you "always take the smaller number away from the larger number." In sixth grade, when positive and negative integers are introduced, students will learn of many situations when a greater number is subtracted from a lesser one.

Do these misconceptions and error patterns occur only in the earliest grades and only with number and operations? Absolutely not! Many students think that all hexagons are yellow and have six sides and angles that are exactly the same size, because the only time they see hexagons is when they are using pattern blocks. This overgeneralization naturally causes problems when these students are asked to create a hexagon, each side of which has a different length.

Commercially made posters available at many teacher supply stores can also support students' misconceptions and overgeneralizations. Many children think that a rectangle *has* to have "two long sides and two short sides," because these are the only examples they see. This becomes a problem in later grades when they are asked to classify a variety of shapes or are told that all squares are rectangles. Many children just don't believe this last statement (and there are adults who don't believe it, either!). Many intermediate students do not believe there are any numbers between zero and one. Few believe there are any numbers between .1 and .2. The examples they have been given (or not given) contribute to these misconceptions.

▣ What You'll Find in This Book

We identify many common errors relative to the five National Council of Teachers of Mathematics (NCTM) content standards (NCTM 2000) and investigate the source of such misunderstandings. If the problem is the result of something said or shown, we propose how to respond and suggest alternate ways to teach the concept so that the misconception can be avoided. If the misconception or error pattern is already ingrained, we share ideas and activities that help "undo" the confusion.

Chapters 1 through 5 delve into the types of misconceptions that children have across each of the five NCTM content standards: number and operations, algebra, geometry, measurement, and data analysis and probability. In these chapters, you will see how things we say and do (or don't do) may impact student understanding. Each chapter includes several classroom vignettes, each of which highlights a common misconception for that particular content area. Following each vignette, we point out the error being made and present some research providing you with a deeper understanding of how commonplace this error is. We then offer reasons for the error and provide you with numerous instructional ideas and activity suggestions that may prevent or remedy the misconception. Finally we pose questions for you to think about on your own or to discuss with colleagues. It is our hope that these questions will guide your reading of this book, allowing you to discuss not only these errors but others your own students are making and why this might be.

Chapter 6 offers assessment ideas (formative and summative) that can be used to quickly assess a student's level of understanding and potential for developing an error pattern or misconception.

▣ Additional Resources

In addition to this book, we have written two activity books—*Activities to Undo Math Misconceptions, Grades PreK–2* for teachers of preK through grade 2, and *Activities to Undo Math Misconceptions, Grades 3–5* for teachers of grades 3 through 5. Each of these books contains teaching suggestions as well as black line masters for more than seventy-five activities (some are referenced in the book you are currently reading, some are not). These activity books give you a concise glimpse at an error pattern and offer you a list of suggestions for eliminating it. Each activity book also comes with a CD-ROM containing editable versions of all of the activities in English and in Spanish. This feature allows you to take our ideas and make them more appropriate for your own students, either by differentiating the level of difficulty or making the situations more relevant to your particular students.

Number and Operations

1

An entire book could be written solely on the overgeneralizations, misconceptions, and error patterns that early childhood and elementary students have about number and computation. *Error Patterns in Computation*, by Robert Ashlock (1994), is just such a book. It presents several examples of a series of error patterns, then asks the reader to figure out what the student is doing (come up with a diagnosis) and think about what a teacher might do to remediate the student's thinking.

Our chapter begins with counting, because children in prekindergarten and kindergarten often forget to include the "teen" designations (thirteen, fourteen, fifteen, and so on). Also, many teachers of young children relate addition to "joining" and subtraction to "separating" and forget that there are other models for each operation. As a result many children get confused when they are asked to find the difference between two sets of objects, answering the "how many more" question with the number of objects in the set that has more. Similarly, open sentences or part-total ideas create problems because they haven't been addressed in earlier instruction.

There are very few second-, third-, and even fourth-grade teachers who don't complain about students' inability to add and subtract multidigit numbers (especially when it involves regrouping and renaming). It's the biggest concern we hear from second-grade teachers who are responsible for introducing these operations to their students. And it's what so many third-grade teachers say they would love students to begin third grade knowing how to do.

Multiplication and division are next. While these operations are predominantly taught in third through fifth grades, younger students are introduced to the ideas behind these areas of computation in story problems. Yet students seem to have a great deal of confusion about how to model both operations and then how to make these computations with multidigit numbers.

And then there are fractions. We could easily have written a dozen segments on the problems that elementary students have understanding what a fractional amount means, forming equivalent fractions and simplifying them, and adding and subtracting fractions. The first fraction that prekindergarten and kindergarten students are exposed to is one-half—a concept that isn't hard for a young child to grasp. It's the introduction of the symbols, too early, that seems to lead to some strange "understandings." Here we deal with forming equivalencies and simplifying to lowest terms, as well as with adding and subtracting fractions.

Finally, we couldn't present a chapter on number and operations without looking at decimal numbers. First graders learn how to write monetary amounts using a decimal point, and by fifth grade, students are adding and subtracting decimals with different place values.

Counting with Number Words

It's the second week of school in a public school in Newark, New Jersey. The kindergarten teachers are doing all sorts of counting activities to determine which students can count in a stable order, which can count rationally (and up to what quantity), and which have "emerging" skills.

In one classroom, Seth is "showing off" his counting skills by determining the number of plastic bears in a bowl. "I can count all these bears!" he announces proudly.

"Let's see how many there are," his teacher responds.

"One, two, three, four, five, six, seven, eight, nine, ten, eleven, twelve, thirteen, fourteen, sixteen, seventeen, eighteen."

"So, how many are there?"

He smiles and says, "There's eighteen."

"Show me again how you figured that out."

As before, Seth counts each bear, picking them up one at a time, and skips over the number fifteen.

Thanking Seth, the teacher asks Marta to figure out how many bears she has in front of her.

"One, two, three, four, five, six, seven, eight, nine, ten, one-teen, two-teen, three-teen, four-teen, five-teen, six-teen, seven-teen, eight-teen, nine-teen." She stops there, even though there are more bears.

"What comes after that?"

"I don't know those numbers yet," Marta says.

Liam has ten bears neatly lined up in front of him. His teacher watches as he points to each one: "One, two, three, four, five, six, se, ven, eight, nine."

"How many bears do you have there?"

"Nine," he says, smiling.

Perhaps the funniest sequence is that of a student who seems extremely confident. She's taken several handfuls of connecting cubes out of the large bag on her table, challenging herself to count to a high number. "One, two, three, four, five, six, seven, eight, nine, ten, tenty-one, tenty-two, tenty-three, tenty-four, tenty-five, tenty-six, tenty-seven, tenty-eight, tenty-nine." Here she stops, even though there are a few more cubes in front of her.

▪▪ *Identifying the Error Patterns*

There is no pattern to be found in the number words one through twelve. Then when students begin counting the "teens," thirteen and fifteen are confusing, because they base their prefix on the ordinal numbers *third* and *fifth*. All the other teen numbers have the cardinal number word in front of the *teen* (for example, *four*teen). Seth skipped fifteen in his number word sequence, counting the set of seventeen plastic teddy bears using one-to-one correspondence, verbally tagging each object with a number word but skipping fifteen. When his teacher asked "So, how many are there?" he responded without recounting, "There's eighteen." This demonstrated that he was developing an understanding of cardinality—that the last number said also represented all those counted before—even though his count was not accurate. When asked to recount, he skipped fifteen again.

Marta was satisfied with the counting sequence she used because it sounded right. She had connected the words from eleven to nineteen in a pattern that made sense. Since all these number words end in *teen*, she overgeneralized the counting pattern and put each number word (from one to nine) in front of the teen numbers, using *threeteen* and *fiveteen* because they sounded like the others.

Liam counted ten teddy bears and got nine. He thought that *se* was one number word and *ven* was the next. His misconception was that number words are one syllable. The number words one through six all have one syllable. And so do eight, nine, and ten. Therefore, his count stopped at nine.

We've all heard children who skip over number words and even return to number words already recited in order to continue their counting sequence. They remember some number words at the beginning of a count, forget some later, and skip ahead to others as their count continues. These students know there is a "word" for each object counted, because they hear and watch their classmates model this very thing daily. However, their inconsistency hinders their ability to count rationally.

▧ *What the Research Says*

Research into young children's understanding of number by the American psychologists Rochel Gelman and C. R. Gallistel (1986) revealed five principles of counting:

1. *One-one principle*. Each item to be counted has a "name," and we count each item only once during the counting process.

2. *Stable-order principle*. Every time the number words are used to count a set of items, the order of the number words does not change.

3. *Cardinal principle*. The last number counted represents the number of items in the set of objects.

4. *Abstraction principle*. "Anything" can be counted and not all the "anythings" need to be of the same type.

5. *Order-irrelevance principle*. We can start to count with any object in a set of objects; we don't have to count from left to right.

▧ *Ideas for Instruction*

A great numbers of books can be used as a springboard for counting activities that enrich students' understanding. The preK–grade 2 and grades 3–5 activity books each include a bibliography of our favorite counting books. Below are some recommended instructional activities and strategies for supporting children's developing ideas about counting, whether they are done with preK students or with students in fourth and fifth grades as they count by fractions and decimal numbers.

► Count out loud often with students. Children count higher when they count together, and they will hear the number word sequence being used correctly.

► Lead children in singing counting songs and chanting counting rhymes. These engaging experiences help them develop rote counting skills and understand the stable-order principle.

► Match the strategy of counting out loud with concrete objects. For example, count the number of students in class by tapping a student on the shoulder as each number word is said. This strategy supports students' understanding of the one-one and stable-order principles.

► Use a circle counting game to help students with the more difficult numbers of eleven, twelve, and those in the teens. Arrange students in a circle and designate a number such as twelve. Students begin to count by ones, and the student who says twelve sits down. The next student begins to count from one again; again, the student who says twelve sits down; and so on (Wright et al. 2006).

► Expect your students to count from a number other than one. For example, ask students to count by ones beginning at six. Initially they may need to whisper one, two, three, four, five before going on. Many opportunities to practice will strengthen their ability to count on immediately rather than beginning at one each time.

► Promote counting on by having students toss a pair of dice and "total" the two numbers. For example, if the number of dots, or *pips*, showing on the top face of one die is five and the other is three, students count on from five saying, "six, seven, eight" (three more numbers) or from three saying, "four, five, six, seven, eight" (five more numbers) to get the total number of pips.

► Provide opportunities for students to count backward using the number word sequence in reverse. Instead of always counting backward from ten, let students count backward from other numbers such as eight.

- ▶ Help students understand the one-one principle of counting by:
  - Letting them use salad tongs to pick up each object as it is counted.
  - Letting them use a stick to point to each object being counted.
  - Giving them an egg carton or ice cube tray and having them place each object being counted in the individual spaces.

- ▶ Help students see the need for keeping track of the individual items being counted. (They should count concrete objects, which they can move, rather than pictures on worksheets, which cannot be moved.) Young children often use the correct number word sequence and tag each object with one-to-one correspondence, but count some of the objects twice, forget to count others, or keep on counting because they haven't kept track. Give students "counting mats" that have a line drawn down the middle so that as each object is counted, they can slide it across the line to the other side. Placing the counted objects in a paper bag reinforces not only keeping track but the stable-order and one-one principles as well. Egg cartons and ice cube trays also help students keep track of objects as they are counted.

- ▶ Help students understand the cardinal principle by asking, "How many?" when students complete a counting task. Another strategy is to count a set of objects together, and at the end of the count repeat the final number: "One, two, three, four, five. There are *five* books."

- ▶ Use number-logic riddles to prompt students to apply critical thinking to the counting sequence. Number-logic riddles progress in difficulty through the counting sequences 1–9, 1–25, 1–50, and 1–100. Sample logic riddles are included in the grades 3–5 activity book (Bamberger and Oberdorf 2010, pages 3–6).

- ▶ Have students count a set of objects in different ways to help them become more flexible in thinking about part-whole relationships. For example, 52 can be shown as 52 singles, 5 tens and 2 singles, or 3 tens and 22 singles. This also helps students connect counting by ones to counting by groups and singles (tens and ones, for example), so they begin to develop an understanding about place value.

▪▪ Questions to Ponder

1. What common path games can help students develop their understanding of the one-one counting principle?

2. What additional activities or strategies can you use to help your students become successful counters?

➕ Thinking Addition Means "Join Together" and Subtraction Means "Take Away"

A small argument is brewing in the corner of Mr. Long's first-grade classroom. Four students who have been given a story problem (Carmen has 9 pennies. Brian has 4 pennies. How many more pennies does Carmen have?) have used four different strategies to get three different answers.

Malik says, "The answer is 9 pennies. If Carmen has 9 pennies and Brian has 4 pennies and you take Brian's 4 pennies away you still have Carmen's 9 pennies!" (See Figure 1–1.)

Hong rolls her eyes and says, "That's just plain wrong. The story says 'more' so you have to add the 9 pennies and the 4 pennies and that means there are 13 pennies. Thirteen pennies is more than 9 or 4 pennies."

Figure 1–1 *Malik models both sets with pennies.*

"But that's not what the story is saying," Kendra insists. "See [using counters to illustrate], here are Carmen's pennies. Here are Brian's pennies. You want to know how many pennies Brian needs to catch up to Carmen. Look, he needs 5 more pennies."

"I got the answer of 5 pennies, too. But that's not how I did it," Simon tells the group. "Here are Carmen's pennies [models 9 pennies with counters]. This is a subtracting story, so you have to take away Brian's 4 pennies. Then there's 5 pennies left. Nine take away 4 leaves 5."

◨ Identifying the Error Patterns

Each student in the above vignette seems to know a strategy for solving a story problem. Three of them use counters to model the problem. Hong has a strategy for figuring out the total of 9 and 4, and knows that in many situations the word *more* cues finding a sum. Simon understands that the problem is suggesting subtraction as the operation with which to solve it, even though his model doesn't directly match the story. Kendra understands that the story is asking for a comparison between two sets. She also models it and demonstrates the difference between Carmen's and Brian's pennies.

Hong has overgeneralized that whenever the word *more* is used in a story problem the operation of addition is required. (Let's assume she got this idea on her own: when addition problems all use the word *more*, it's very easy to do.)

Malik's error is the most interesting. He understands the problem and even models the two sets of pennies. But he's heard the phrase *take away* too often, so he does this and removes Brian's 4 pennies. If he had recorded 9 − 4 = ___ on paper, he probably wouldn't have said the answer was 9. With the models in front of him, however, it was easy for him to believe that removing Brian's 4 pennies still left Carmen's 9 pennies.

Simon certainly gets the correct answer of 5. But his explanation makes it clear that he has a misconception that with all subtraction there is taking away. Since he believes the story calls for subtraction, the only recourse he has is to take away 4 counters.

◨ What the Research Says

Carpenter and Moser investigated students' strategies for solving different types of addition and subtraction story problems and the impact these strategies had on teachers' instructional decisions. They determined that young children were able to solve a variety of story problems using strategies that ranged from modeling the problem with counters (including fingers) to recalling basic facts or using derived facts (Carpenter and Moser 1983; Carpenter, Carey, and Kouba 1990). In addition, these researchers identified a hierarchy of problem types—join problems, separate problems, part-part-whole problems, and compare problems—that were more or less complex. For a useful summary of the problem types, see Van de Walle and Lovin (2006, 144).

Below are four story problems that must be solved by subtraction; however, the semantic equation (the equation based on the structure of the story)—and therefore the level of difficulty—is different for each, and "take away" makes sense only for the first:

1. *Separate: result unknown.*

   Jon had 7 gumballs. He gave 2 to his sister. How many gumballs does he have now?

   Semantic equation: $7 - 2 =$ ___

2. *Join: change unknown.*

   Jon had 2 gumballs. How many more does he need to have 7 altogether?

   Semantic equation: $2 +$ ___ $= 7$

3. *Part-part-whole: part unknown.*

   Jon has some red gumballs and 2 blue gumballs. He has 7 gumballs altogether. How many red gumballs does he have?

   Semantic equation: ___ $+ 2 = 7$

4. *Compare: difference unknown.*

   Jon has 7 gumballs. His sister has 2 gumballs. How many more gumballs does Jon have than his sister?

   Semantic equation: $7 - 2 =$ ___

▪▪ *Ideas for Instruction*

Prekindergarten and kindergarten teachers can do many things to ensure that students do not enter first grade with misconceptions and overgeneralizations about addition and subtraction. An obvious one, to prevent the misconception that subtraction means "take away," is to be sure to use the word *minus* or *subtract* when referring to the subtraction symbol and to reinforce this when students read their equations. Another is to give students many opportunities to take apart a set of objects and put it back together again, perhaps using Cuisenaire® Rods or bicolored counters.

In *Developing Number Concepts Using Unifix Cubes* (1984), Kathy Richardson provides many open-ended problem-based activities that give students a sense that a quantity can be represented in a variety of ways.

Introducing the following activities provides students the opportunity to see that quantities can be represented in many different ways:

▶ Give prekindergarten or kindergarten students two colors of cubes (the quantity depends on the number being learned) and ask them to represent this number in different ways. If 6 is the number being worked on, children get 12 cubes, 6 of one color and 6 of another color. (All students have the same two colors.) Students also have many blank six-square grids (see Figure 1–2) on which they can place the cubes in various configurations. (They can color in the squares to document each arrangement.) Afterward the students as a class see how many different configurations were created. This activity reinforces the notion of part-part-whole for both addition and subtraction.

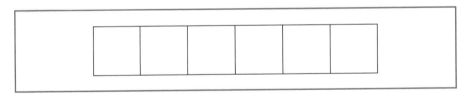

Figure 1–2 *Blank Six-Square Grid*

▶ Give prekindergarten or kindergarten students a specific number of cubes or tiles (all the same color) and have them arrange them on a twenty-five-square grid (see Figure 1–3) in various ways. The grid in Figure 1–3 shows one way to make five. Describing it, a student might say, "I put 2 in the top row, 2 in the second row, and 1 in the third row to make my 5." Another student might describe this same arrangement as, "I put 1 in the first column, 2 in the second column, and 2 in the third column to make 5 altogether." Sharing ways to make a specific number is an important precursor to later work with addition and subtraction.

▶ Have prekindergarten students sort a limited set of dominoes (total number of pips per block from zero to six) in order to explore various ways of representing a specific amount. (A full set of double-six dominoes can be used with

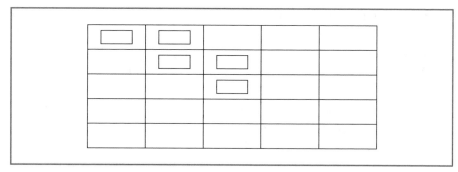

Figure 1–3 *Grid with Arrangement for the Quantity of Six*

kindergartners.) By first grade, students are familiar with different ways to visualize quantities and they can think of part-whole ideas, not just joining and separating relationships. Sample domino problems are included in the grades preK–2 activity book (see Figure 1–4).

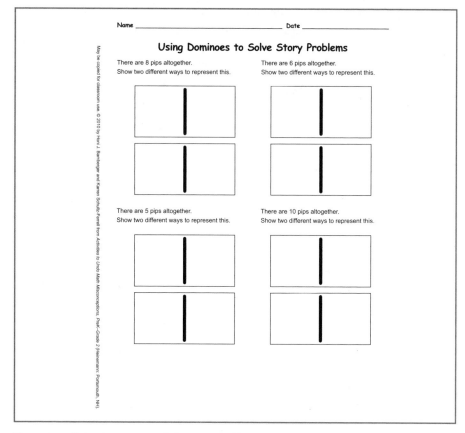

Figure 1–4 *Using Dominoes to Solve Story Problems*

▶ Even prekindergarten students can solve simple context-related story problems. For example, if the class keeps track of the date using a calendar, you can ask, "Today is Tuesday, February 3rd. How many more days until it's the 5th?" Or, "We've been in school for 97 days; how many days until the 100th day?"

▶ In either prekindergarten or kindergarten, use a yes/no graph (see Figure 1–5) to help students think about comparative subtraction ideas even before symbolic representations are used. If the question of the day is, "Do you have the letter *a* in your first name?" have children put their clothespins on either the yes side or the no side of the graph. Then you can ask, "How many people are on the yes side? How many people are on the no side? How many more people are there on the yes side?"

▶ In first grade, you can incorporate all sorts of appropriate addition and subtraction story problems into your instruction. *How Many Snails?* (1994), by Paul Giganti, has pictures on each page that students can use to practice counting, naming attributes, determining part-whole relationships, and performing comparative subtraction. Looking at the very first page you could ask, "How many

YES	NO
• 18	18 •
• 17	17 •
• 16	16 •
• 15	15 •
• 14	14 •
• 13	13 •
• 12	12 •
• 11	11 •
• 10	10 •
• 9	9 •
• 8	8 •
• 7	7 •
• 6	6 •
• 5	5 •
• 4	4 •
• 3	3 •
• 2	2 •
• 1	1 •

Figure 1–5 *Yes/No Graph*

MATH MISCONCEPTIONS

clouds do you see? How many clouds are gray? How many clouds are white? How many clouds are small? How many clouds are large? Think of a number sentence that could be used with this picture." Make sure the numbers match up with the illustration. When numbers are attached to illustrations, the notion of parts and wholes becomes more real to students. Subtraction stories could also be created that show comparisons: *There are 8 clouds in the sky; 4 of them are white and the others are gray. How many gray clouds are there?*

▶ In first and second grade, present a variety of problem types and structures to help students move away from the overgeneralization that adding means joining and subtracting means taking away.

▪▪ *Questions to Ponder*

1. What manipulatives do you currently have to reinforce the idea of part-whole for addition and subtraction?

2. How might you communicate to families the way you'll be teaching the concepts of addition and subtraction so that misconceptions and overgeneralizations about addition and subtraction do not occur?

➕ Renaming and Regrouping When Adding and Subtracting Two-Digit Numbers

Mr. Walters has worked hard during the first half of the school year to make sure his second graders understand different ways to represent two-digit numbers. They've played games using a hundreds chart and solved story problems using different strategies. Today, as a preassessment, he's given them the following story problem:

> Janet and her dad baked cookies for the class bake sale. On Saturday morning they baked 2 dozen cookies. In the afternoon, they baked 3 dozen cookies. How many cookies will Janet bring to the bake sale?

He's also provided craft sticks, rubber bands, connecting cubes, a hundreds chart, number lines, and paper and pencils for students to use to help them solve the problems.

Most of the students know that a dozen cookies means 12, and those that don't ask someone for help. However, their answers include 5 dozen, 50, 60, and 510. The students who answer 5 dozen don't know how many individual cookies that equals.

Mr. Walters asks the four students who got 50 as their answer to share how they got it. Here's their strategy: "There are 24 cookies in 2 dozen and 36 cookies in 3 dozen. We wrote the 24 over top of the 36. We added 4 plus 6 and that equals 10. Since you can't have more than 1 digit in a place we just put the zero in the answer. Then we added 2 tens plus 3 tens and that equals 5 tens. So, the answer is 50."

Next, Mr. Walters asks Christian and Marcel to explain what they did to get their answer of 510. "We used connecting cubes and paper and pencil. First, we made 2 stacks of 10 and 4 ones for the 2 dozen cookies. Then we made 3 stacks of 10 and 6 ones for the 3 dozen cookies. We put the ones together and that equaled 10 ones. We put the tens together and that equaled 5 tens."

Another pair of students says, "We put together stacks of cubes, too, but after we put the ones together we knew that we could make a stack of 10 with them. Then we had 6 tens altogether. The answer is 60."

Mr. Walters says, "Looks like we have different answers to this story problem, and we'll need to figure out which one is right."

▪▪ *Identifying the Error Patterns*

These students struggle with place value. To get the answer *510*, the sum of the ones and the sum of the tens were recorded without regard to place value. In another story problem, for which they got 14 as the difference between 54 and 48, students weren't looking at 54 as the total amount and 48 as one part of this total amount. Instead, they thought about each digit in the numerals, subtracting the lesser digit from the greater digit regardless of its place in the expression. (It's also possible that students who understood the idea of commutativity in addition thought it applied to subtraction as well.)

▪▪ *What the Research Says*

"When children focus on following the steps taught traditionally, they usually pay no attention to the quantities and don't even consider whether or not their answers make sense" (Richardson 1999, 100). Sad but true. We know our students need to learn how to compute. We also know that an understanding of place value in our numeration system is critical to computing efficiently and effectively. Yet teaching so that students can understand the traditional algorithm seems to be a real challenge.

Children are already using two-digit numbers in kindergarten. They count sets of objects greater than nine and often are able to count from one to a hundred by rote. However, their understanding of quantity is based on a "one-more-than or count-by-ones approach" (Van de Walle and Lovin 2006, 188). Asked to determine the quantity of thirty-two counters, they count by ones. Seldom, if ever, will they use any grouping skill (unless they are sorting by color at the same time they are counting). For students to understand place value, they need to connect the concept of grouping by tens with the procedure of how to record numerals based on this system of counting.

Counting is fundamental to constructing an understanding of base-ten concepts and procedures. Asking early elementary students to count quantities of objects in several different ways is a good first step in helping them make sense of place value (Thompson 1990). This may mean, in early instruction, asking, "Would you still have 32 if you counted these by twos instead of by ones? By fives? By tens?" "Making a transition from viewing 'ten' as simply the accumulation of ten ones to seeing it both as ten ones and as one ten is an important first step for students toward understanding the structure of the base-ten number system" (Cobb and Wheatley 1988).

By counting objects first by ones, then grouping objects and checking to see that the quantity remains the same, and finally grouping by tens with ones "left over," students acquire the necessary conceptual skills for understanding place value and get a clearer sense of how to rename numbers (when subtracting) or regroup them (when adding) when using the traditional or an invented algorithm. Procedural connections, in which students write the matching numerals, decompose the quantity in a variety of ways, write the corresponding equivalencies, and then practice saying the equivalencies, enable them to move from merely being able to identify the digit in the tens and ones place to making sense out of the quantity of groups of tens and ones in a numeral.

Models that are both proportional and groupable should be used before models that are proportional but not groupable. These first models include connecting cubes, connecting links, sticks that can be banded, and counters that fit in a cup. It is easy for students to put these things together and take them apart and see that thirty-two can be:

■ Thirty-two separate counters

■ Three groups of 10 counters and 2 single ones

- Two groups of 10 counters and 12 single ones

- One group of 10 counters and 22 single ones

"Given the opportunity, children can and do invent increasingly efficient mental-arithmetic procedures when they see a connection between their existing count-by-tens knowledge and addition by ten" (Baroody and Standifer 1993, 92).

When to formally introduce students to multidigit written arithmetic remains unclear (Baroody 1990). While manipulative models can help students understand multidigit numbers, they don't guarantee that students will understand a formal algorithm. Many mathematics educators recommend spending a good deal of time with manipulative models while simultaneously practicing mental computation before putting pencil to paper to solve expressions (Baroody and Standifer 1993, 92).

■■ *Ideas for Instruction*

The activities below can help students make sense out of tens and ones as well as represent tens and ones symbolically. These experiences will better prepare them to compute with two-digit numbers. Some of these activities can be done with prekindergartners and kindergartners; others are more appropriate for first and second graders. They can be used with the whole class, in small groups, or in learning centers. Decide which ones will work best for your students based on their current understanding.

▶ Post a hundreds chart in a prominent place in the classroom and put an individual copy on each student's desk. Ask students to look for patterns they notice on the chart. Talk about these patterns and ask students questions that will develop their relational understanding of these numbers:

- Put your finger on the number 46. What number comes just before 46? What number comes right after 46?

- What number is 10 more than 46? What number is 10 less than 46?

- What are some numbers that are greater than 46? What are some numbers that are less than 46? Are these numbers a lot less/greater than 46 or a little bit less/greater than 46?

▶ Create puzzles out of hundreds charts. Ask students to cut charts apart in different ways, put them back together, and explain (orally or in writing) how they knew where each piece went.

▶ Ask students to look at a hundreds chart and figure out how many rows of 10 are in the number 46 and how many extra ones there are.

▶ Play Make 100 (see the preK–grade 2 activity book). This game lets students practice their basic addition facts (1 + 1 through 6 + 6) and reinforces the concept of tens and ones in two-digit numbers. Materials needed are a bicolored mat; a pair of numeral cubes in a covered transparent cup; connecting cubes or links (or sticks with bands); and a recording sheet for each student. Each student, in turn, tosses the cubes inside the cup, states the sum of the two numbers, takes that number of counters, and keeps a record of the sums tossed and the number of cubes (tens and ones) on his or her mat. Play ends after the twelfth turn; students determine how close they are to one hundred. Be sure to connect the game and the concepts of tens and ones, recording two-digit numerals, and addition. For example, if a student has 2 tens and 8 ones on her mat and then tosses the cubes to produce a sum of 9, you could ask the following series of questions:

■ When you took those 9 cubes, where did you place them?

■ If you put them on the ones side, did you then have more than 9 ones altogether?

■ What did you have to do with those 17 single cubes?

■ When you made your stack of 10 cubes and had 7 cubes left as ones, did you still have 17? (This is probably *the* question that trips students up. If the student says yes, ask her to prove it to everyone in the group. Many students think 17 ones are not the same as 1 ten and 7 ones.)

■ Now, how many tens do you have on your mat and how many ones?

■ How many total cubes are on your mat now?

▶ Play Get to Zero (see the preK–grade 2 activity book). This game is the reverse of Get to 100, but rather than beginning with one hundred (a three-digit number) students begin with 9 ten-unit counters on their mat. They again toss two numeral cubes and state the sum, but this time this quantity is removed from the mat. On the first turn, students need to rename their 9 ten-unit groups as 8 tens and 10 ones or 7 tens and 20 ones: there's no way to remove between 2 and 12 cubes without breaking apart 1 or 2 groups of 10 and making them into ones. Information is recorded on a recording sheet, and play continues for ten turns. (Is it possible to get to 0 from 90 in 10 turns, using two cubes with the numbers 1 through 6? Yes, but only if a student gets a lot of sums that are greater than 9—a great discussion to have after students have played this game several times.)

▶ Have students, using counters (tiles, cubes, sticks, whatever) and bicolored mats, represent any two-digit number using groups of tens and ones only. Then ask them to think of a different way to record this same number, still using tens and ones only. Take the number 72, for example. Many children will make 7 groups of 10 with 2 single ones and record this as 7 tens and 2 ones. Now they have to think about another way to record 72 using tens and ones only. Some may break apart another group of 10, which results in 6 tens and 12 ones. Once students check to be sure they still have 72 cubes, they may realize they can break other tens into ones. Keeping a record of these ways to show 72 creates a chart on which students can identify patterns (see Figure 1–6).

After you've done these activities and others, you can introduce computation with an expression that allows for a variety of ways to solve it. Ask students to figure out the sum for "the double of 28." After they've done so, ask them to share their strategies while you record them symbolically. Here are some strategies second graders typically use:

■ I wrote 28 + 28 and knew that the first 28 was only 2 away from 30. So I took 2 away from the second 28 and gave it to the first 28. Then I had 30 + 26 and that was easy to solve. The sum is 56.

Figure 1–6 *Ways of Representing the Quantity 72*

Tens	Ones
7	2
6	12
5	22
4	32
3	42
2	52
1	62
0	72

- I knew that 20 + 20 equaled 40 and that 8 + 8 equaled 16. And 40 + 16 equals 56.

- I knew that 28 + 20 equals 48. Then I just counted on 8 more to get 56.

- I knew that 30 + 30 equals 60. Each 30 is 2 more than the 28, so I had to think 4 less than 60. That's 56.

Students need to see that there are multiple ways to get a sum when adding, even if your school insists that the traditional algorithm be taught. To teach the traditional algorithm, begin with models, move on to a pictorial representation, and use symbols only when it's clear that students understand that 16 ones is the same as 1 ten in the tens place with the remaining ones in the ones place. Label the place values instead of saying digits.

Most textbooks separate subtraction with renaming from subtraction without renaming, but this isn't necessary. In fact, it's probably not a good idea, because students will try to guess whether "this is the kind of problem where you have to rename." Introduce subtraction computation the same way you did addition. Use the hundreds chart to look for patterns, play Get to Zero, and have students explore expressions for which there are multiple ways to get the difference. Here are examples of how students approached the expression 51 – 19 = ___:

- I thought 51 minus 20 and that's 31. But it's really only 19, so I had to add that 1 back. The answer is 32.

- I thought 50 minus 20. That's easy; it's 30. But I changed the 51 by 1 and the 19 by 1 so I have to add 2 back to 30. That's 32.

- I thought 51 minus 10. That's 41. Then I just counted back 9 to 32. You never have to count back more than 9.

There are many ways to arrive at the difference between two numbers. If the traditional algorithm needs to be taught, ask the following questions so the numerals are being looked at, not just the digits:

- Is it possible to take 19 away from 51? How do you know this?

- If you have 1 one, can you take 9 ones away? Where could you get more ones without changing the 51?

- If you've renamed the 51 to 4 tens and 11 ones, do you still have 51? How could you prove this?

- Now, how would you subtract 19 from your 4 tens and 11 ones?

What's great is that students can now work from left to right, rather than from right to left. And if students leave second grade truly understanding two-digit numbers and how to operate on them, third-grade teachers will be ecstatic.

Questions to Ponder

1. What other hundreds-chart activities help students better understand two-digit numbers?

2. What other manipulative materials help students add and subtract? How can you use them?

3. How can you use estimation activities to reinforce ideas of tens and ones?

4. What research supports your instruction of place value, addition, and subtraction?

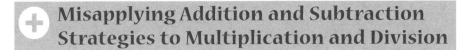

Misapplying Addition and Subtraction Strategies to Multiplication and Division

Ms. Elliott's third graders recognize the inherent connections between addition and multiplication. Her class has used various strategies to solve multiplication problems and record multiple representations. Some students have drawn arrays, while others have shown equal "hops" along a number line. They have written multiplication equations as repeated addition problems. These experiences have vividly illustrated the notion of multiplication as repeated addition. It's time to apply that initial understanding of multiplication to a different type of problem. Ms. Elliott writes the following multiplication problem on the board and invites her students to find a solution:

$$57 \times 6 = \boxed{}$$

As the students talk with one another and compare the strategies they used to reach their solutions, Jenny looks at Evan's paper and says, "That's not the answer I got; my answer is smaller. I know that 57 equals 50 plus 7, so I did 50 times 6 plus 7 times 6 and I added them together. My answer is 300 plus 42, or 342." Evan looks puzzled. Jenny's explanation makes sense, but he feels confident in his strategy and answer as well. (See Figure 1–7.)

Figure 1–7 *Jenny and Evan's Work*

Jenny's Work	Evan's Work
57×6	57×6
$57 = 50 + 7$	57 rounds to 60
$50 \times 6 = 300$	$60 \times 6 = 360$
$7 \times 6 = + 42$	$- 3$
342	357

Evan says, "I think my answer is right. Look, when I do addition with big numbers, I sometimes round up to make the numbers easier to do in my head. I did the same thing this time. If it was addition, I would change the 57 to a 60, add 6 to find the sum, and then take out the 3 that I added to the 57 at the beginning when I rounded to 60. So for this problem, I rounded 57 to 60 and multiplied 60 times 6. I got 360. Then I took out the 3 that I added to change the 57 to 60. I got 357 for my answer."

▌▌ Identifying the Error Patterns

What did Evan do wrong? Why couldn't Jenny pinpoint why Evan's answer was incorrect even though she strongly believed her answer was right? If Evan's strategy worked for addition and if multiplication is repeated addition, why didn't it work for this multiplication problem? Rounding 57 to 60 was an efficient step in solving this problem. Multiplying 60 by 6 was also a logical next step. The error occurred when Evan attempted to readjust the estimated product to arrive at the final answer. He knew he needed to modify the answer by subtracting 3, since he added 3 to the initial value; his misconception was not realizing he had to subtract 6 threes, not just 1 three, because he had changed the 57 to 60 six times over.

▌▌ What the Research Says

Principles and Standards for School Mathematics (NCTM 2000) identifies multiplicative reasoning as one of the central themes for grades 3 through 5:

> In grades 3–5, multiplicative reasoning emerges and should be discussed and developed through the study of many different mathematical topics.

Students' understanding of the base-ten number system is deepened as they come to understand its multiplicative structure. That is, 484 is 4×100 plus 8×10 plus 4×1 as well as a collection of 484 individual objects. (144)

This example illustrates the connection among multiplication, division, and place value and reinforces how such connections work to empower students with understanding. *PSSM* also describes the effectiveness of using rectangular arrays as a geometric model. Additionally, Graeber and Campbell (1993) suggest that a visual area model makes the commutative property of multiplication more apparent and contributes to students' ability to compose and decompose numbers.

Ideas for Instruction

Ms. Elliott will want to reinforce some key concepts to ensure her students understand multiplication and division. Strategies include:

▶ Use a number line. (Using rulers, yardsticks, and meter sticks instead of premade paper number lines reinforces the operations while also highlighting the connection of multiplication and division to measurement.) Figure 1–8 describes some possible movements up and down the number line.

Figure 1–8 *Using Number Lines*

Using Number Lines

Tools	Description	Result
12-inch ruler, counter	Show 3 hops of 3 inches each.	Moved 9 inches total.
Yardstick, pipe cleaners	Display the number of 3-inch hops (multiples of 3) you must make to reach the end of the yardstick (36 inches). Make each hop with a pipe cleaner.	12 pipe cleaners are placed on the yardstick, one every 3 inches.
Meter stick, pipe cleaners	Divide the meter stick into 4 equal parts. Mark each section with a pipe cleaner.	Each section is 25 centimeters. The pipe cleaners are placed on the 25 cm, 50 cm, and 75 cm marks.

▶ Play Equal Groupings (see the grades 3–5 activity book). Students use a spinner and die to generate two multiplication factors and then draw a representation and record the equation.

▶ Play Equal Groupings with dividends and divisors.

▶ Introduce a partial products strategy where students model the operation of the multiplier on both the tens and ones value of the multiplicand, thus considering the value of the whole number rather than the individual digits [for example, $32 \times 41 = (30 \times 40) + (30 \times 1) + (2 \times 40) + (2 \times 1)$].

▶ Use the area model to help students see yet another representation of their multiplication expressions (see Figure 1–9). Have students use base-ten blocks on centimeter grid paper to construct rectangular arrays to represent the problem (see the grades 3–5 activity book).

Figure 1–9 *Evan Building Rectangular Array*

1. Which multiplication and division strategies maintain the emphasis of place value? Which do not?

2. When teaching multiplication and division, how do you decide which models and representations to use so that students understand the multiplicative concept?

 ## Multiplying Two-Digit Factors by Two-Digit Factors

Micah has been given twenty multidigit multiplication expressions to complete for homework and has done most of them incorrectly. He repeatedly makes errors when he encounters a two-digit multiplicand and a two-digit multiplier. Below are just three examples:

$$
\begin{array}{r} 56 \\ \times\,23 \\ \hline 118 \end{array}
\qquad
\begin{array}{r} 71 \\ \times\,52 \\ \hline 352 \end{array}
\qquad
\begin{array}{r} 48 \\ \times\,36 \\ \hline 168 \end{array}
$$

However, he's done $356 \times 8 =$ ___ correctly, so his teacher asks him to explain his process.

"First you start in the one's place. Eight times 6 equals 48, and you put the 8 down here and carry the 4. Eight times 5 equals 40, plus the 4 equals 44. You put the 4 down here and you carry the other 4. Then it's 8 times 3 and that equals 24 plus the 4 equals 28. So you write the whole 28 down here because there aren't any other numbers to multiply."

"So what is the product of 356 and 8?"

"The answer is 2,848," Micah says tentatively.

"Does that answer make sense to you? Does it sound like it would be the correct answer to 8 groups of 356?"

"I guess," Micah says, the expression on his face clearly indicating his uncertainty.

"It's definitely right!" his teacher says encouragingly. "When I think about whether it makes sense, I think that 8 three hundreds is twenty-four hundred, or two thousand four hundred. Since the first factor is greater than 300, the product should be greater than 2,400, but still sort of close. So to me your answer makes sense."

▪▪ *Identifying the Error Patterns*

Micah seems to know his basic multiplication facts. And, for the most part, he remembers that you don't record the entire partial product beneath the line. The tens digit gets regrouped into the tens place. So far, so good. He also seems to know that you need to "use" all the digits in the problem. In the first of his incorrect examples, he uses both the 3 and the 2 in 23 and the 6 and the 5 in 56.

Unfortunately, he treats each numeral as a digit, not realizing that the 2 in the 23 really means 20 and the 5 in the 56 really means 50. He first multiplies the 3 times the 6 and gets 18 as the partial product. He records the 8 and regroups the 1 (ten). Then he multiplies the 2 times the 5 and gets 10 as the product. He adds the regrouped 1 to the 10 and records 11. He doesn't think about whether this makes sense as a possible answer. He just moves on to the next example.

▪▪ *What the Research Says*

While specific research on multiplication of two-digit by two-digit factors is limited, several mathematics educators have discussed errors in multiplication computation and reasons for these errors. In *Error Patterns in Computation*, Robert Ashlock describes the error made by Micah as a "blend of the algorithm for multiplying by a one-digit multiplier and the conventional addition algorithm" (Ashlock 1994). Students spend a good deal of time learning and then practicing multidigit addition. Consequently, it's not uncommon that they combine algorithms when they do not have a complete understanding of place value (decomposing numbers) as well as what it means to multiply.

Ruth Stavy and Dina Tirosh, in *How Students (Mis-)Understand Science and Mathematics* (2000), attribute an error of this sort as one based on "intuitive rules." Schemas about concepts and procedures are formed by students. Without a firm understanding of new content, students return to "relevant intuitive rules" that they have come to rely on. These may not make sense in the specific situation that they are now in, but unless new knowledge makes sense these rules persist.

Finally, Jae-Meen Baek spent time with students in six classrooms in grades 3–5 to observe the different algorithms that were invented, as well as to see whether students were utilizing the traditional algorithm. Since none of the teachers taught rules or formal algorithms to students, many developed procedures that made sense to them. Students were observed adjusting numbers, drawing pictures, directly modeling, and partitioning numbers. "Many children in the study developed their invented algorithms for multi-digit multiplication problems in a sequence from *direct modeling* to *complete number* to *partitioning numbers into non-decade numbers* to *partitioning numbers into decade numbers*" (Baek 1998, 160). Not only does this observation lead one to believe that multidigit multiplication algorithms can be invented by students, but it also leads one to believe that when this is done students have a clearer understanding of how to multiply.

■■ *Ideas for Instruction*

Common error patterns can be avoided if multiplication problems are introduced in a way that emphasizes making sense. It's much easier to teach something effectively the first time than to try to undo teaching that has led to errors.

We can assume that second graders have learned the repeated addition model for multiplication. Maybe they've played games or used materials to represent problems of this sort. Second graders see multiplication as "important mathematics" and are motivated to learn about it because it's "what older kids learn." "Schooling builds on students' intuitive understanding of addition and subtraction by focusing on additive situations in the early grades and then introducing situations that can be addressed through multiplicative reasoning in the later grades" (Chapin and Johnson 2000, 61).

But multiplication is far more complex than just repeated addition. Here are some helpful approaches you can use to nurture this understanding:

- Use rectangular arrays as models. They can be linked to repeated addition.

- Model cross-product problems using arrays that illustrate the commutativity and the distributive properties of multiplication. An array provides a visual model of the multiplication algorithm even when both factors are two-digit numbers. It often makes believers out of students who are struggling with the traditional procedure, since it models each partial product.

- Begin with a story problem to give a context for the numbers and help students realize that mathematics is necessary in the world as well as in school.

Here's a detailed example of how to approach a story problem. First, here's the problem:

> The school cafeteria is being set up for the choral assembly to be performed on Monday night. Eighteen chairs are in each of 21 rows. How many people will have seats at this performance?

Before dismissing pairs to work on a solution, trigger a brief discussion using the following questions:

- What do you picture, in your mind, given the details of this story?

- If there was only 1 row of 18 chairs, how many total chairs would there be?

- What if there were 2 rows? How many chairs would there be? What did you do to get this answer?

- Can you figure out how many chairs there would be if there were 10 rows with 18 chairs in each row?

- Can you make an estimate about the number of chairs there would be in 21 rows?

Give the student pairs centimeter grid paper, connecting cubes, square tiles, base-ten blocks, and chart paper to display their final answer and the strategy that was used to get the answer.

Students could use centimeter grid paper to outline an 18-unit by 21-unit rectangle and then figure out a strategy for counting the number of squares. Students wanting to "build" the array with square tiles or connecting cubes would also need some strategy for determining the total amount. Base-ten blocks are an efficient method for modeling the factors and each partial product, as well as displaying the product in an easy-to-see way. (See Figure 1–10.)

Once all pairs have displayed what they've done on chart paper, ask different pairs to share what they did to get their answer. Make sure a variety of strategies are represented. Ask students which strategies took a long time to work through. Those who outlined an 18-unit by 21-unit rectangular grid probably found it tedious to figure out the total number of square units. This would also be the case for those who built the rectangle with square tiles and/or connecting cubes. Since strategies involving symbols, drawings, and/or base-ten materials are more efficient, have students practice them.

Here is a strategy that clearly demonstrates an understanding of the place value nature of each factor; decomposing each factor makes it simpler to compute:

$$36 \times 27$$
$$30 \times 20 = 600$$
$$30 \times 7 = 210$$
$$6 \times 20 = 120$$
$$6 \times 7 = \underline{\ 42\ }$$
$$972$$

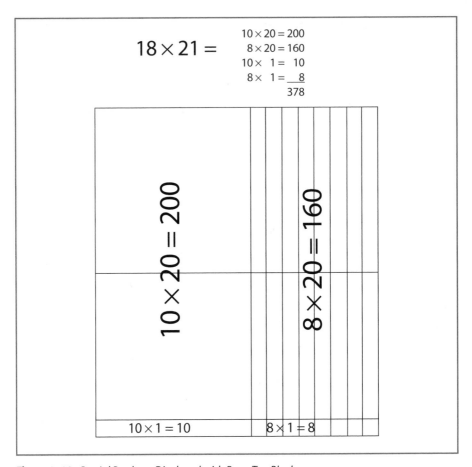

$18 \times 21 =$

$$10 \times 20 = 200$$
$$8 \times 20 = 160$$
$$10 \times 1 = 10$$
$$8 \times 1 = \underline{8}$$
$$378$$

$10 \times 20 = 200$

$8 \times 20 = 160$

$10 \times 1 = 10$ $8 \times 1 = 8$

Figure 1–10 *Partial Products Displayed with Base-Ten Blocks*

By thinking of the factor 36 as 30 + 6 and the factor 27 as 20 + 7, students begin to realize that each of the "parts" need to be multiplied in order for the product to be correct.

Another efficient procedure is to cut out one of the above steps and think of this particular problem as:

$$36 \times 20 = 720$$
$$30 \times 7 = 210$$
$$6 \times 7 = \underline{42}$$
$$972$$

Making sure that these algorithms are displayed and discussed ensures that students have a clearer sense of what is happening when factors that have more than one digit are being multiplied.

1. What are some other common errors students make when multiplying multi-digit numbers?

2. What are some effective strategies that you've used to help students understand why their procedures aren't yielding the correct answers?

✚ Understanding the Division Algorithm

Ms. Waters is beginning her unit on long division, something she dreads. First she asks her students to share what they know about division. Most are able to give good examples about sharing things fairly so everyone gets the same amount. Some are even able to name the different parts of the division equation: dividend, divisor, and quotient. Next she presents the following story problem to the entire class:

> Miranda baked 72 cupcakes. She wants to share these with her 2 sisters so the 3 girls can each bring an equal amount to school for the bake sale. How many cupcakes will each girl get?

Ms. Waters hopes her students will be able to relate to this scenario and have some idea of what the answer might be. She asks them to guess the number of cupcakes each girl will take to school.

"It's going to be more than 20, since 20 times 3 equals 60 and there are 72 cupcakes," Larry offers.

"That's a great way to think about this problem. Do you think that it will be more than 25?"

"It can't be 25, because that's like three quarters and three quarters is 75 cents. But there aren't 75 cupcakes," Mellissa says.

"It's more than 20 but less than 25 cupcakes," Michael says emphatically. "So it could be 21, 22, 23, or 24."

Everyone in the class agrees. The estimation skills they've been working on seem strong and they understand the meaning of division.

"Let's look at the procedure that people use to solve a problem like this. We know it's a division problem because the cupcakes are being shared equally among three children. What's the divisor in this problem?"

Brian says the divisor is 3 because that's the number of children sharing the cupcakes.

Ms. Waters then asks the children what the dividend is. In unison the students say, "Seventy-two." Ms. Waters sets up the problem and talks out loud as she solves it (see Figure 1–11).

"Here's what you'll be doing. You say to yourself, how many times does 3 go into 7? It goes into 7 two times and the 2 is placed up above the 7 like this. You have just divided. The next step is to multiply. Two times 3 is 6 and that gets written down below the 7. The third step is to subtract the 6 from the 7 and that leaves 1. Finally you bring down the 2 and now you have 12 and you start the procedure all over again. First you divide 3 into 12. That's 4, which you put next to the 2. Then you multiply the 4 times the 3 and that's 12. You write the 12 underneath this 12 and when you subtract, 0 is the difference. You have nothing left to bring down so the division is finished. What is the final answer?"

No one raises his or her hand. Ms. Waters says, "The answer is up here at the top. Remember you said that it would be greater than 20 but less than 25. What is it?"

Several students put their hands in the air and tentatively answer, "Twenty-four," the question in their voices indicating they aren't sure.

"You just have to follow the steps. Remember? Divide, multiply, subtract, bring down—D, M, S, B. Dead Monkeys Smell Bad." The expressions on the faces of these fourth graders make it clear that none of this, especially the mnemonic, makes any sense to them.

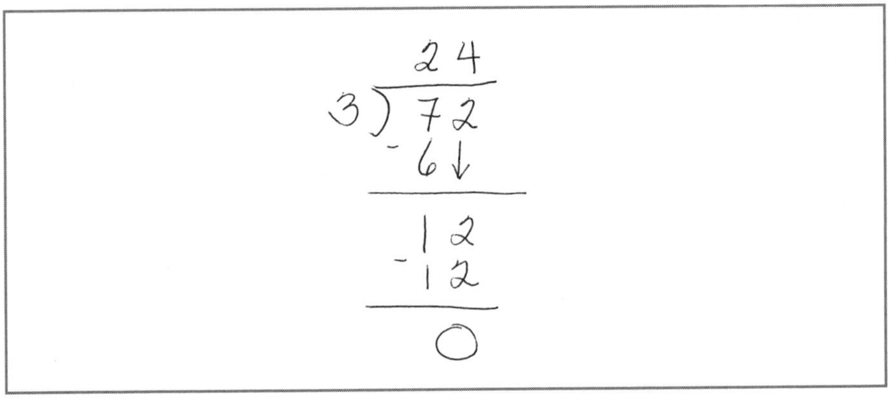

Figure 1–11 *Division Using Traditional Bracket*

Ms. Waters then calls the names of eight students to join her at the circle table while the other students complete a review sheet with addition, subtraction, and multiplication facts. She gives the eight children at the table the following problem:

> Sheri is sharing her bag of candy with 11 of her friends. She's getting some candy, too. When she counted the candies she found out that there were 254 candies in the bag. How many candies will each person get? If there is any leftover candy what will Sheri do with them?

Lydia reads the problem out loud, and Ms. Waters asks the same sorts of questions she asked during whole-group instruction. Students know the divisor is 12 and the dividend is 254, and the story makes sense to them. When Ms. Waters asks what the answer might be, it's a good minute before anyone speaks. Finally Renee says, "Ten twelves equal 120 and 20 twelves equal 240. The answer has to be close to 20, just like the problem we did in class!"

"That's kind of a coincidence," Ms. Waters says. She doesn't want students to make an overgeneralization that you'll always get a quotient that is around 20 when dividing. "Let's set up the problem the way I did on the board and I'll talk you through the steps."

After talking through and working two more problems together, the students return to their seats to try the following problem independently: 3,208 ÷ 8. Daniel, whose work is shown in Figure 1–12, comes up with the quotient of 41.

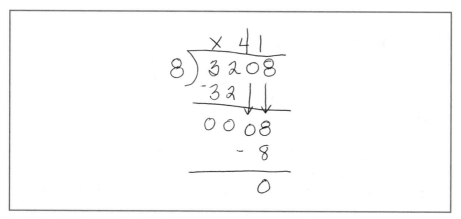

Figure 1–12 *Daniel's Quotient of 41*

■■ *Identifying the Error Patterns*

Daniel's error is very common, and it probably stems from the way the traditional algorithm is taught and the words that are used. Daniel probably said to himself, "Eight doesn't go into 3, but it goes into 32 four times. Eight doesn't go into 0, but it goes into 8 one time. Eight goes into 3,208 forty-one times." Done! But doesn't 8 divide into 3,000? That's what that the 3 really means. And 8 definitely divides into 3200— exactly 400 times. If Daniel were saying these sorts of things rather than, "Eight goes into," he would have realized that an answer of 41 is absurd. He looked at digits while dividing, rather than the actual numeral that was being divided.

■■ *What the Research Says*

"The traditional long-division algorithm is difficult for many students. Many never master it in elementary school and fewer develop meaning for the procedure or the answer" (Silver, Shapiro, and Deutsch 1993). There are many reasons for this. First of all, the procedure contains so many steps, and for each step students need to get an exact answer in the quotient.

Another reason is that the algorithm treats the dividend as a set of digits rather than an entire numeral. Students are taught to ignore place value as they routinely work through a procedure they don't necessarily understand. In the above vignette, Ms. Waters asks her students to think of how many threes there are in 7 rather than how many threes there are in 70. As a result they lose all sense of the complete number and rely on their memory of a series of rote steps. "The standard algorithm works against students' number sense" (Carroll and Porter 1997, 371).

■■ *Ideas for Instruction*

Once students have a strong conceptual understanding of division and understand the relationship between multiplication and division, they are ready to work through a computation procedure. But must we teach our students the traditional algorithm? Many teachers feel we must. We say we don't. If a student is able to develop a procedure for dividing that is efficient, effective, and generalizable, it's perfectly fine for them to use it.

An efficient procedure works without too many steps. If a student draws 72 cupcakes and then draws lines, one at a time, to 3 girls, she may get the correct answer but the procedure is not efficient. The same would be true if the student wrote 72 ÷ 3 = ____ and then subtracted 3 from 72 until there was nothing left and counted up the number of threes subtracted. An algorithm is effective if the correct answer is obtained every time. And an algorithm is generalizable if it "can be applied to the full range of problems of the type being solved" (Campbell, Rowan, and Suarez 1998, 53).

Here are some things teachers can do to help their students understand long division and make correct computations:

▶ Provide a variety of engaging, realistic story problems. Problems involving both the partitive model and the measurement model provide students with a clearer understanding. Here are some examples:

> Brittany is making beaded bracelets for her girlfriends. She bought 2,000 beads to use. She knows that each bracelet needs 85 beads. How many bracelets can she make?
>
> Marcus wants to share his baseball card collection with his 3 best friends. He has 281 cards in his collection. How many cards will each friend get?
>
> Each drink booth at the school's May Fair needs a large bag of ice cubes. A bag can hold 90 cubes. The school's ice machine made 4,300 cubes. How many booths will get ice?
>
> Lauren has collected 3,857 pennies. She is going to roll up these pennies and cash them in for bills. A roll of pennies has 50 pennies. How many rolls of pennies will she make? How many dollars will she get for these rolls?

▶ Have students write and solve their own story problems.

▶ Provide students with manipulative materials to model the story but have them also record what they've done symbolically. When the numbers get too large for individual counters, base-ten materials, Digi-Blocks®, and banded craft sticks can represent numbers larger than 100 quite easily.

▶ Ask students to share the strategies they used to get their answers and then discuss whether these answers make sense. Students create the most amazing algorithms. Fourth-grader Marianna used this one to solve $4,327 \div 5$:

$4,327 \div 5 = 800$	"4,327 divided by 5 equals 800. But 800 times 5
$\underline{4,000}$	is really 4000. You still have 327 to divide by 5.
$327 \div 5 = 60$	327 divided by 5 equals 60. But 60 times 5 is really
$\underline{300}$	300 so you still have 27 to divide by 5. That's just a
$27 \div 5 = 5$ r 2	basic fact with a leftover. The answer is 865 r 2."
865 r 2	

Her algorithm works every time and is extremely efficient. It relies on having a good sense of number and being able to use multiples of ten, one hundred, and even one thousand.

▶ Look at ways to adjust numbers to make them easier to use. Let's look at the expression 1430 ÷ 5. We don't have to use an algorithm to do this problem; we only need to understand how to divide by 10. If we double the divisor from 5 to 10 and then double the dividend from 1,430 to 2,860 the balance within the expression remains the same and the quotient is easy to compute. (See the grades 3–5 activity book for additional examples.)

▪▪ *Questions to Ponder*

1. How do you help students move from representing a division problem with manipulative materials to using a paper-and-pencil algorithm?

2. How do you get a student who has an effective but inefficient algorithm to adopt one that is more efficient?

➕ Understanding Fractions

"Your teacher invited me to bring a snack to all of you today, but she didn't tell me how many boys and girls were in your class," the classroom visitor says anxiously.

"We have 21 kids in our class," one student offers.

"This is a real problem. I baked corn muffins and brought apple juice for you to eat and drink. And Ms. Pryse and Ms. Robles will want a snack, right? Come to think of it, I'm hungry, too. But I know that I didn't bake 24 muffins."

"Maybe everybody could get a part of the muffin," suggests Joey.

"That's a great idea. And I have plenty of paper cups because I bought a whole package. So maybe everyone can get part of a cup of juice."

The visitor removes napkins, home-baked corn muffins, bottles of apple juice, paper cups, and dull plastic knives from a shopping bag and asks the children to help figure out how many muffins there are. "What can we do to figure out how many muffins I baked?"

"We can count them!" shout a chorus of children. Everyone counts together and finds there are exactly 12 muffins.

"Is that enough for everyone to get a muffin?"

Students look around at their classmates and begin to count.

"Twelve is at Jacob," Mara says. "Everybody isn't going to get a whole muffin."

"Well, Joey said that everybody could get a part of a muffin. How can we do this so it's fair?" the visitor asks. She draws a circle on the whiteboard and tells the children to pretend it's a corn muffin. Then she draws a line so that one part is large and the other is small. "If we cut the muffin this way, would that be okay?" (See Figure 1–13.)

"You have to put the line in the middle," Arlene volunteers. "Then both of the parts will be the same."

The visitor draws a circle of the same size next to the previous one and bisects it exactly in half. The children clap. "That's fair, isn't it? How many parts are there?"

"Two."

"And what do you notice about these parts?"

"They're the same."

"The parts are the same size, aren't they? Each of those parts is one-half of the whole muffin. If everyone gets one-half of a muffin I'm pretty sure I'll have enough muffins for everyone. Everyone will get half of a muffin."

"I want the bigger half," Anthony says.

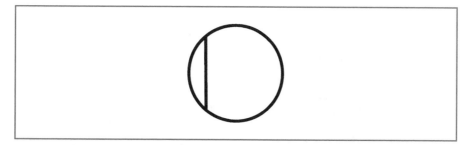

Figure 1–13 *Circle Divided into Two Unequal Pieces*

▚ *Identifying the Error Patterns*

Anthony's "I want the bigger half" is a typical response from young children, who have differing interpretations of what *half* means. They begin to encounter fractions informally before they start school. Unfortunately, they often either see incorrect models or hear fractional relationships being used incorrectly. How often does a parent separate a cookie into two different sizes and offer a child the *bigger half?* The child ends up thinking of a half as any part of a whole instead of one of two equal parts and sees the "half" of the cookie taken as being larger than the "half" of the cookie remaining.

Misunderstandings about the size of a fraction may also result when something being shared (a corn muffin, for example) is difficult to divide equally. Students need many informal chances to divide a variety of objects into equal parts and then compare these parts to each other directly.

Fiona Lawton (2005) describes additional common misconceptions that children have in the primary grades:

- *Dividing a nontraditional shape into parts such as thirds.* (See Figure 1–14.)

- Children who are only used to dividing traditional shapes such as squares, circles, or rectangles into equal parts begin to think that the way they divide these shapes will work for all shapes.

- *Identifying a fraction of a set.* (See Figure 1–15.)

  In this example, the child doesn't recognize the entire set of animals as a whole unit. He compares the two cats in the set to the four dogs and incorrectly identifies ²⁄₄ of the animals as cats.

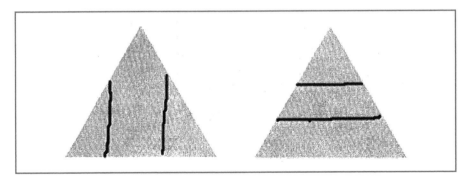

Figure 1–14 *Equilateral Triangle Divided into Three Unequal Parts*

Figure 1–15 $^2/_4$ *of These Animals Are Cats*

■ *Making sense of fractional names and vocabulary.* The top number in a fraction is the counting number and counts the parts or shares. The bottom number tells what fractional part is being counted (for example, in $^4/_5$, *fifths* are being counted). It is not unusual for a child to identify one-half of a shape as *one twoth*, which makes perfect sense: she is trying to apply a consistent naming system to a system that isn't consistent.

■ *Ranking written fractions.* Children frequently choose $^1/_4$ as larger than $^1/_3$, over-generalizing what they know about whole numbers and applying it to comparing and ordering fractions. They do not yet understand that the larger the denominator, the smaller each of the equal parts in the whole, which is a major idea in the learning of fractional concepts.

What the Research Says

Sherman, Richardson, and Yard (2005) suggest several reasons for students' difficulties in learning about fractional concepts and skills:

■ They memorize procedures and rules before they have developed a conceptual understanding of the related concepts.

- Early instruction in mathematics focuses on whole numbers so children over-generalize what they know about whole-number computation and apply this knowledge to fractions.

- Estimating rational numbers is more difficult than estimating whole numbers.

- Recording fractional notation is difficult and confusing for students if they do not yet understand what the top and bottom numbers represent. Knowing which is the numerator and which is the denominator and what those numbers mean is critical. It is important that we build on children's intuitive understandings and help them make sense of ideas encountered before entering school.

Chapin and Johnson (2000) list four critical interpretations of fractions necessary for computing successfully:

- *Part of a whole or parts of a set.* An object can be separated into two or more equal parts, and a specific number of objects in a set can represent a fractional amount.

- *Fractions as a result of dividing two numbers.* An example of this method is the number of apples each child receives when ten apples are shared among two children.

- *Fractions as the ratio of two quantities.* A ratio of 2:10, for example, might represent the comparison of two cats with a total of ten animals and is a fraction that tells what part of the set are cats ($^2/_{10}$).

- *Fractions as operators.*

"Research supports the idea that the part-whole interpretation, which involves partitioning wholes into equal-size pieces and identifying the different-size units, is the best way to approach learning about fractions in the early grades; the other interpretations are introduced later in elementary and middle school and build on students' initial understanding of part-whole relationships" (Chapin and Johnson 2000, 75).

Ideas for Instruction

"Children need many opportunities to talk about fractional parts, see examples, work with concrete materials, and relate these experiences to the standard mathematical notation. Such experiences are best done over time, so that children can develop familiarity and understanding" (Burns 2000, 224). To help students develop a deeper understanding of fractional concepts you can:

▶ Explore the concept of *fair shares*. Students' intuitive understanding about fair shares may be incomplete when they enter school and need clarification.

▶ Provide opportunities to share a variety of objects, so that children become more flexible in their thinking about fractions. While it makes sense to divide a circle, a square, or a rectangle fairly in initial experiences, eventually present other types of shapes for students to divide. This will prevent children from overgeneralizing that all kinds of shapes can be divided in the same way.

▶ Introduce the vocabulary of fractional parts after students have explored a fractional situation. In the early grades, just name the parts; don't introduce the symbolism. For example, when a square has been divided into four equal parts, simply say, "We call these *fourths*. The whole is cut into four parts. All of the parts are the same size—fourths" (Van de Walle and Lovin 2006, 254).

▶ Introduce fractional concepts in the context of things other than pizza! In an activity included in the preK–grade 2 activity book, a pan of brownies is divided into halves in different ways. (See Figure 1–16.)

    Children typically begin by dividing the pan of brownies down the middle, either horizontally or vertically. However, they soon realize that the brownies can be divided into halves in any two groupings of an equal number of equal-sized pieces. Equal parts do not always have to look the same, but they must have the same number of equal-size units, the same area, or the same volume. (Grid paper also allows students to explore this idea.)

▶ Expose students to more than just halves, thirds, and fourths. An activity included in the grades 3–5 activity book presents directions for folding a triangle into eighths. When the triangle has been folded in half three times, let students count the fractional parts in the triangle (one-eighth, two-eighths, three-eighths, four-eighths, and so on).

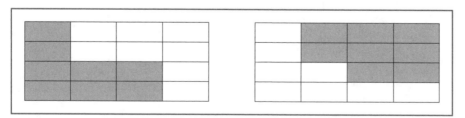

Figure 1–16 *Halves That Are Not Congruent*

▶ Provide opportunities for students to count fractional parts. A Days of the Week fraction bar is included in the grades 3–5 activity book.

Questions to Ponder

1. What specific difficulty have your students had or what overgeneralization have they made about fractions this year? Discuss this misconception with members of your teaching team or with an instructional support teacher.

2. How will you plan instruction so that students can develop a better understanding of this fractional concept?

Adding and Subtracting Fractions

Ms. Hampton's class has just begun adding and subtracting fractions with like denominators. She gives them the following story problem in order to assess their understanding:

> For the summer picnic, Mr. Phelps baked a pan of brownies that he cut into 8 equal-size parts. Before he arrived at the picnic he noticed that $^3/_8$ of the pieces were missing. Mr. Phelps figured (correctly) that his 3 children had each had a brownie! Then he decided he should try the brownies himself to make sure they tasted all right. Mr. Phelps ate another $^2/_8$ of the pan. What fractional part of the pan has already been eaten? What fractional part of the pan does he now have to bring to the picnic?

Many students draw pictures of a rectangular pan split into 8 fairly congruent pieces; first they split the pan in half (either horizontally or vertically) and then split the halves into fourths the opposite way (see Figure 1–17).

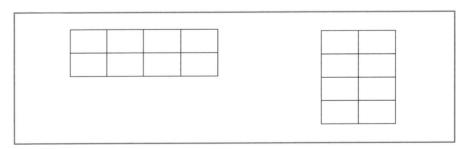

Figure 1–17 *Pan of Brownies Split into Eighths*

Some children shade 3 of the pieces in 1 color, then 2 more pieces in a different color; some put Xs over 5 of the 8 pieces; and some just shade 5 pieces the same color. Based on these illustrations, all the students seem to understand that $5/8$ of the brownies have been eaten, leaving $3/8$ of the pan to bring to the picnic.

However, this isn't what their equations show: more than half the students have written $3/8 + 2/8 = 5/16$. Furthermore, no one seems to be bothered that there are two different answers.

"So what's the answer to the story problem? Is it $5/8$ or $5/16$?" Ms. Hampton asks.

"It's $5/8$ when you show it with a picture," Jamal says, "but it's $5/16$ when you show it only with numbers."

"Is it possible for a story problem to have two different answers?"

Some students nod yes, others shake their heads no, still others seemed totally confused by the discussion.

Identifying the Error Patterns

First and second graders learn how to add and subtract with whole numbers. Typically children are exposed to single-digit addition of two addends in grade 1 and then two-digit addition and addition with multiple single-digit addends in grade 2. And they get plenty of practice. It's no wonder that many of them use this procedure later when adding fractions. They remind themselves to "add each digit." Each part of the fraction is treated as a different single-digit whole number. The numerators are seen as whole numbers and are added together. The denominators are also seen as whole numbers and are added together.

What the Research Says

"In terms of instructional approaches, lessons are too often focused on procedures and memorizing rules rather than on developing conceptual foundations prior to skill building" (Sherman, Richardson, and Yard 2005, 139). This is one reason offered by the authors to explain why students experience difficulties when learning rational number skills and concepts. Many researchers have concluded that the complex topic of fractions is more challenging for elementary students than any other area of mathematics (Bezuk and Bieck 1993).

Before students study how to add and subtract fractions, they need to understand the meaning of fractions through various models, as well as how to use the language of fractions. Watanabe (2002, 457) delineates three models frequently used in elementary textbooks and school curriculums—the linear model, the area model, and the discrete model (often referred to as the set model). Van de Walle (2007) provides some important "big ideas" that children often confuse. For computational understanding, it is critical that students know that:

■ Fractional parts are equal-size portions or equal shares of a whole or unit. (Many students think that the parts have to look the same, when it's really the size of the part that has to be the same).

■ The special names for the numbers that make up a fraction tell how many equal-size parts make up the whole (the *denominator*) and how many of the fractional parts are being considered (the *numerator*).

The National Mathematics Advisory Panel (2008) notes that one key instructional strategy to link conceptual and procedural knowledge of fractions is the ability to represent fractions on a number line.

▪▪ *Ideas for Instruction*

Here are some things a third-, fourth-, or fifth-grade teacher can do to make sure that computation with fractions is learned correctly:

► Introduce activities in which children count by fractions. Begin by using mathematics materials with which children are already familiar—pattern blocks, for example. If a yellow hexagon represents one whole, the trapezoid is one-half of this whole. (See the "Counting Fractions" activity found in *Activities to Undo Math Misconceptions, Grades PreK–2.*)

► Have students combine their "fraction kits" (see *Activities to Undo Math Misconceptions, PreK–2*) so they can count by halves, thirds, fourths, sixths, eighths, and even twelfths. If they get good at this, ask them to combine strips from their kit: "If you have 5 of the one-twelfth pieces and you add 2 more one-twelfth pieces, what fraction will you now have?" Be careful to ask the right question. The answer to "How many pieces do you have now?" is 7—not the answer you want.

▶ Introduce story problems that reinforce what it means to add and subtract fractions. (See "Apple Surprise" in *Activities to Undo Math Misconceptions, Grades 3–5*.) Don't have students record the equation until they have shared their strategies for getting their answers. As students share their solutions and strategies, write the corresponding equation for them to see. Once students have been introduced to a number of examples ask, "What do you notice about how fractions are added or subtracted when the denominators are the same?" Most students will have noticed that the numerators are added or subtracted but the denominators stay the same. Asking "Why do you think that this happens?" reinforces the fact that if you have eighths and add more eighths, you'll end up with even more eighths. It just makes sense.

▶ Use the number line to represent fractions. The number line is an effective tool for comparing the magnitude of fractions as well as adding and subtracting fractions with like denominators.

▦ *Questions to Ponder*

1 What big ideas about fractions must students understand before they are able to build a conceptual knowledge of equivalence?

2. What opportunities or supports can you use to empower students to manipulate values by using their own number sense rather than simply relying on procedures?

✚ Representing, Ordering, and Adding/Subtracting Decimals

Ms. Foley administered a preassessment to her fifth graders in preparation for a unit on decimals. The formative task included the values 0.4, 0.23, and 1.0 and required students to:

■ represent the decimal fractions in word form

■ shade in a representation of each value

■ order the decimals from least to greatest

■ find the sum of all three values

■ find the difference between any two values

While the class worked independently on the task, Ms. Foley circulated from student to student noting relevant observations about their performance. She was surprised by the number of students incorrectly recording the word name for each decimal fraction. Nearly half of the class recorded a literal translation of the symbols (zero point four) rather than a word form representing the value (four-tenths).

Rowan seemed confused when representing 0.4 on the 10 × 10 grid. He shaded in 4 of the 100 boxes, but it was evident by his expression he was not satisfied with his answer.

"Rowan, remember that the 10 × 10 grid represents one whole," stated Ms. Foley. Rowan did not change his answer. Ms. Foley wondered what kind of representations Rowan had experienced in the past, and began thinking about how she might address this instructionally.

Thomas ordered the decimals showing 0.4 with the least value and 1.0 with the greatest value. When asked why he thought that 0.4 was less than 0.23, he explained that 23 is bigger than 4.

Jeanne set up the addition problem and calculated a sum of .37. Ms. Foley asked Jeanne why she set up the problem as she did.

"You always line up the digits from right to left and then add in that order, too."

She continued, "The first decimal point I come to is the one in 0.23 so I put it in that same spot in the answer."

Neal chose the values 0.4 and 1.0 to find the difference, setting the problem up with 0.4 as the minuend and 1.0 as the subtrahend. He wrote positive 3.0 as his answer and told Ms. Foley that the 0 in 0.4 didn't mean anything so he subtracted 1 from 4 and got an answer of 3.

A summary of Ms. Foley's observations are included in Figure 1–18. She collected a lot of information regarding students' current level of understanding and would use these anecdotal notes to plan effectively for the decimal unit.

▪▪ *Identifying the Error Patterns*

The first error revealed on the preassessment is related to naming decimal fractions. While many students did write the correct word form (four-tenths and twenty-three-hundredths), many others were unable to provide the correct word form.

Figure 1–18 *Samples of Student Errors*

Samples of Student Errors

	0.4	0.23	1.0
Word Form	• zero point four	• Point twenty-three • two-tenths and three-hundredths	• one point zero
Representations			
Rankings	Thomas This is the least because it is less than one whole and smaller than 0.23 because it has fewer numbers than 0.23.	Miranda This has the greatest value because it has 3 digits and the others only have 2.	Natasha This is the smallest because 1 is less than 4 and 23. You just look at the numbers since they all have a decimal point.
Addition Errors	Jeanne 0.4 0.2 3 + 1.0 0.3 7	Sasha .4 1.0 + 2.3 7.3	Simon 1 plus .4 equals 1.4, so 1.4 + .2 3 3.7 I don't know where the decimal goes.
Subtraction Errors	Sarah 0.4 − 1.0 3.0	Chris 1.0 − 0.23 1 .23	Neal 0.4 − 0.23 0.23

For the visual representation, the 10 × 10 grid is defined as one whole. In the first example, Rowan shaded in four hundredths instead of four tenths. Alisha shaded in two boxes in the first column and three boxes in the second column, showing she understood that each digit in .23 held a different value; however, she didn't grasp the relation of the decimal expression to the whole. In the last example, the student drew one whole as one-tenth.

When ordering the decimals from least to greatest, additional gaps in student understanding were revealed. Thomas knew that both decimal values were less than

1.0 but resorted to counting digits as a strategy for ranking the remaining decimals. Some students ranked the value based solely on the number of digits—the longer the number, the greater the value. Others treated all the numbers as whole numbers in assigning value, ignoring the decimal completely.

When adding and subtracting, Jeanne applied rules she'd learned when doing whole-number operations. Others set up the numbers in order to make the computation more doable (without regard for the value). All these errors reveal an emphasis on digits and procedures rather than values and number sense.

In the first addition example, Jeanne aligned all the digits to the right and then added each digit. Sasha aligned all the numbers to the left. Simon began by writing that he knew 1 plus .4 equaled 1.4, but he didn't know how to combine one and four-tenths with twenty-three-hundredths. He lined up the digits as one would with whole-number addition, added them, and lamented not knowing where to place the decimal point. All of these student work samples reveal deficiencies in understanding place value.

In the first subtraction example, Sarah arranged the numbers to subtract the smaller digit from the larger and ignored place value. Chris lined up the decimal points correctly to subtract twenty-three-hundredths from one but then *added* the digits. In the third example, a student set the problem up but only subtracted the digits in the tenth place, not certain what to do with the digit in the hundredths place, so he ignored it.

All of the incorrect responses indicated that students were focused on procedures and did not apply number sense, estimation, or place value to their calculations.

▪▪ *What the Research Says*

A simple yet powerful introduction to decimals is to ask students to represent two related decimal numbers using several representative models (Van de Walle and Lovin 2006). For example, 0.8 and 0.08 could be shown (and ultimately compared) on number lines and 10×10 grids as well as by using coins and base-ten materials or Digi-Blocks®.

Chapin and Johnson (2000) state, "Finding examples of decimals (5.2 on an odometer, say), explaining what the decimal numeral means in the context of its use (I traveled 5.2 miles to work), indicating the general value of the decimal numeral (I live a little more than 5 miles from work), and then stating what two whole numbers the decimal is between (5.2 miles is between 5 miles and 6 miles) helps students recognize that the decimal amount is the sum of a whole number and a number less than one" (99). This approach reaffirms the importance of avoiding "naked" mathematics and instead teaching skills and concepts within a context. Decimal number sense should be a focus during instruction so that students recognize an unreasonable answer (Sherman, Richardson, and Yard 2005). In addition, the decimals used in computation problems should be used authentically—examples include money, the radio dial, linear measure, and digital speedometers.

Ideas for Instruction

Decimal fractions are introduced in the intermediate grades of elementary school. In middle school, students should be able to use decimal numbers to solve problems, make sense of answers, understand scientific notation, and compute accurately. To attain this goal, we need to strive for conceptual understanding that connects the notation with the value being represented. Additionally, we want to help students make generalizations regarding decimal fraction computation. To that end, we can:

▶ *Name the decimal fraction correctly.* It may be tempting to take shortcuts, but teachers need to name these values consistently and appropriately, thus reinforcing the place value. The words "one and seventy-three-hundredths" convey more meaning than "one point seventy-three." Equally important, the word *and* must only be used to indicate the decimal point in a mixed decimal: one hundred twenty-four and one-half, not one hundred *and* twenty-four and one-half.

▶ *Use a variety of concrete models to represent decimal fractions.* Encountering many types of representations helps students focus on the similarities among models, which strengthens their understanding of key ideas.
  ■ Base-ten blocks are commonly used to represent decimal fractions. When using base-ten materials, students have options in naming the value of a given block in order to represent a quantity. For example, when representing whole numbers, the 10×10 block holds a value of one hundred. That same block could be assigned the value of one whole to enable the other blocks to represent tenths and hundredths. Or the block used to represent one thousand when representing a whole number could be assigned the value of one whole, providing representations for tenths, hundredths, and thousandths.
  ■ Another effective model to use with decimal fractions is money. Most fourth and fifth graders have paid cash for things and received change, so this model is effective when comparing quantities including tenths and hundredths. Relating a quantity to money can provide a visual reference for students that makes comparisons and computation more meaningful.

Figure 1–19 *Place Value Chart*

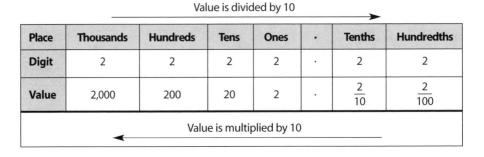

Value is divided by 10 →

Place	Thousands	Hundreds	Tens	Ones	•	Tenths	Hundredths
Digit	2	2	2	2	•	2	2
Value	2,000	200	20	2	•	$\frac{2}{10}$	$\frac{2}{100}$

← Value is multiplied by 10

- A meter stick is another tool students may use to represent decimal quantities, because it has decimeter and centimeter divisions. The meter stick also makes a nice connection between decimal fractions and measurement.

- Digi-Blocks® are commercially made materials designed to show a numeric representation from ten thousand through hundredths. The hundredths pieces are quite small. These materials give students a rare opportunity to model a number as large as 98,765.43, creating a comprehensive visual display that effectively models the value of each digit as well as the entire quantity.

▶ *Provide opportunities to reinforce place value.* Place value is the cornerstone of student understanding of decimal fractions. Students must have opportunities to learn that decimal fractions are an extension of whole numbers on the place value chart and thus recognize the relationship between any two adjacent places in a numeral (see Figure 1–19). The place to the left is worth ten times more than the place to the right. Conversely, the place to the right is worth just one-tenth as much as the place on the left.

Questions to Ponder

1. How can you reinforce the notion that the quantity represented by a digit is the product of its face value and its place value?

2. What comparisons would you expect students to identify between operations with whole numbers and operations with decimal numbers?

Algebra

2

Teachers are often amazed that algebra or algebraic thinking is part of the early childhood and elementary school curriculum. However, because college admission can hinge on proficiency with algebra, teachers at every grade need to foster algebraic thinking and reasoning. By asking elementary school students to share strategies used to solve specific types of problems, teachers provide all students with the opportunity to develop higher-order thinking.

The initial focus is patterns. In prekindergarten the emphasis is on having "children recognize and duplicate simple sequential patterns" (NCTM 2006, 11). As students progress through the grades, these ideas become more complex and detailed. Kindergartners are expected to be able to extend simple number patterns as well as more challenging repeating patterns. In first and second grade, patterns are used to develop strategies for basic facts and properties of numbers and operations. Being able to recognize patterns enables fifth graders to write and solve simple equations and inequalities. "Observations of patterns and relationships lie at the heart of acquiring deep understanding in many areas of mathematics—algebra and function in particular" (Steen 1988).

A foundational algebraic idea is the equality relationship, which is represented by the equals sign. Students must learn that the equals sign represents a quantitative and balanced relationship—that the expression to the left of the equals sign represents the same quantity as the expression to the right. The equals sign means "is the same as" rather than "the answer is." Without a solid understanding of this idea, students find it very difficult to work with equations in which there are unknowns on both sides of the equals sign (New Zealand Council for Educational Research 2008).

In his "President's Message" Henry S. Kepner, Jr., summarized the NCTM's position on algebra and algebraic reasoning as "building conceptual understanding, procedural skills, and problem-solving simultaneously." Our role as educators is to help students and their families better understand that algebra is not just about factoring and solving equations. Algebra is a "tool for understanding and describing relationships" in a variety of settings and being able to represent these relationships and others in many ways. "Knowing algebra opens doors and expands opportunities, instilling a broad range of mathematical ideas that are useful in many professions and careers. All students should have access to algebra and support for learning it" (NCTM 2006, 2).

Understanding Patterns

In the second week of September, Ms. Oblitas begins a lesson on growing patterns. "Who remembers what a pattern is?" she asks her second graders. Nearly every hand goes up, and she calls on Luis, who says, "It's like a banana, apple, banana, apple. That's a pattern."

"That is a pattern," Ms. Oblitas agrees. "Who has a different example or a definition of what a pattern is?" After several children volunteer additional examples of an AB pattern, Ms. Oblitas asks, "Are you only allowed to have two different things in a pattern?" More hands go up and students offer examples of two, three, four, or more units that repeat.

Next Ms. Oblitas gives her students a story problem to solve with a partner (see *Activities to Undo Math Misconceptions, Grades PreK–2*): "Julio got 1 jellybean on Sunday, 2 on Monday, 3 on Tuesday. Figure out how many jellybeans Julio will have at the end of the week." The children use counters as they work and record their answer and the thinking behind it. Moving about the room, Ms. Oblitas notices that student pairs are getting one of two answers, either 13 or the correct answer of 28. She calls the class back to the rug, asking them to bring their papers with them.

Susana and Eduardo explain their answer first. "The pattern is a 1, 2, 3 pattern. On Sunday Julio got 1 jellybean, on Monday he got 2, on Tuesday he got 3, then on Wednesday he got 1 again, on Thursday he got 2 again, on Friday he got 3 again, and on Saturday he got 1. We used counters to show the jellybeans and then we counted them up. There were 13 jellybeans altogether on Saturday."

▪▪ *Identifying the Error Pattern*

Susana and Eduardo, along with many other students, had created a repeating pattern using the core units (1, 2, 3) stated in the problem (see Figures 2–1a and b).

However, other students had figured out that the pattern grew by 1 jellybean each day (see Figure 2–1b).

Because Ms. Oblitas hadn't shown the students any examples of this sort of growing pattern, she asked how they knew this was happening. Timmy said, "Me and Carla weren't sure, but we saw that Julio kept getting 1 more jellybean. So we thought that every day he'd get 1 more. We filled in our week and then added up the numbers."

▪▪ *What the Research Says*

"When students identify patterns furnished by the teacher, books, or the classroom environment or when they memorize—store various patterns and recall them—they internalize the concept of pattern and realize that it is the same irrespective of the changes in the periodic themes that create different patterns" (Hershkowitz and Markovits 2002, 169). This important idea later translates into students' ability to identify functions and numeric and geometric patterns.

▪▪ *Ideas for Instruction*

Identifying and extending simple repeating patterns is part of every kindergarten program, and we want these four- and five-year-olds to continue to experience this important kind of algebraic thinking. But we also want them to realize that the counting sequence is another type of a pattern—for example, counting by ones to 31; by twos, beginning with 2, to 20; by fives, beginning with 5, to 100; and by

Figure 2–1a *Students' Repeating Pattern*

Sunday	Monday	Tuesday	Wednesday	Thursday	Friday	Saturday
1	2	3	1	2	3	1

Figure 2–1b *Students' Growing Pattern*

Sunday	Monday	Tuesday	Wednesday	Thursday	Friday	Saturday
1	2	3	4	5	6	7

tens, beginning with 10, to 100. (Older students also learn to count by fractions, noting patterns as they do so.) Here are some ways to encourage children's thinking about patterns:

▶ Make students aware that there are patterns that repeat as well as patterns that grow. This should begin as early as kindergarten and continue through the grades. Once kindergartners are able to use colored tiles, multilink cubes, or teddy bear counters to identify, extend, and create repeating patterns in which color is the attribute that changes, teachers should write the following sequences and have students say what comes next and then describe the pattern they're seeing:

1, 2, 3, 4, __, __, __, 8, 9, 10, 11

5, 6, 7, 8, 9, __, __, 12, __, 14, 15

10, 9, 8, 7, 6, __, __, __, 2, 1, 0

See Figure 2–2 for a few examples of patterns for students to complete.

Activities to Undo Math Misconceptions, Grades PreK–2 and *Activities to Undo Math Misconceptions, Grades 3–5* suggest other patterns to complete (Bamberger and Oberdorf 2010, pages 43–45).

▶ Have third graders write their first name on grid paper, one letter per square, over and over until the grid is filled. Then ask them to color in the squares using a different color for each letter but keeping every repetition of a letter the same color. (See *Activities to Undo Math Misconceptions, Grades 3–5,* page 46.)

▶ Present fourth and fifth graders with more challenging repeating patterns (those that include different attributes beyond color and shape), as well as numeric patterns involving decimals and fractions. Counting by decimal fractions and common fractions is an important number and operations skill. For example:

½, 1, 1½, 2, 2½, ____, ____, ____, ____

.25, .50, .75, 1.00, 1.25, ____, ____, ____, ____, 2.50, 2.75, 3.0

⅓, ⅔, ⅗, ⁴⁄₃, ____, ____, ____, ⁸⁄₃, ⁹⁄₃, ____, ____

▶ Have students look for patterns in materials they see every day. For example, as they study the monthly calendar, how do they figure out what the date will be a week from today or determine what the date was a week ago? Some students

MATH MISCONCEPTIONS

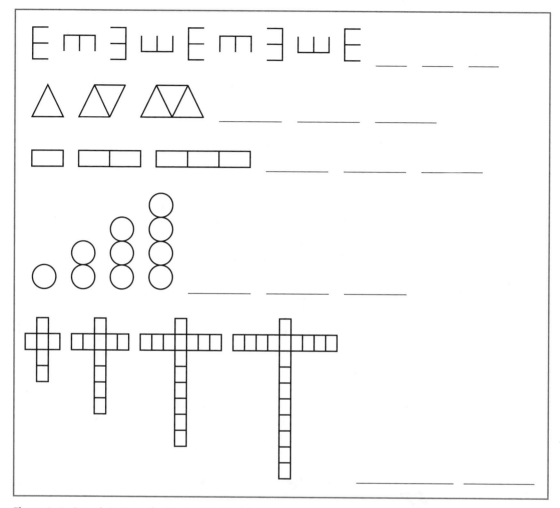

Figure 2–2 *Sample Patterns for Students to Complete*

will realize that determining the date a week ago and a week from today involves counting 7 less or 7 more. Others will discover that looking at the date exactly above and below gives them the answer. No matter how these questions are solved, students notice a pattern. Students can also recognize patterns on a hundreds chart by coloring:

Multiples of specific numbers.

Numbers whose digits sum to 7 (16, 25, 34, …).

Two-digit numbers in which the difference between the digits is 1 (12, 23, 34, 45, …).

Two-digit numbers in which the difference between the digits is 0 (11, 22, 33, …).

- Integrate science and social studies into mathematics by introducing students to patterns that appear in nature and within their environment. Ask,

  "Do you notice any patterns related to the animals we've been studying?"

  "Which of these flowers have patterns in their leaves or petals?"

  "How do architects and planners use information about traffic patterns to determine how roads, homes, and office buildings should be incorporated into their plans?"

  "How do meteorologists use weather patterns to prepare their predictions about the weather?"

- Art and music are also rich with patterns. Emphasize rhythmic patterns in music classes. When students learn about artists, encourage them to look for patterns the artists use within their work.

- Introduce games and activities that need patterns in order to complete the task and/or win the game. The Tower of Hanoi puzzle (see Figure 2–3) requires that discs be moved from one side (pole) to the other pole in the fewest possible moves. Let's look at how this is done, and the rules for solving this puzzle.

  If only one disc is used (it could be on the right pole and needs to be moved to the left pole) it takes one move to go from the right pole to the left pole. (The player is allowed to "jump over" the middle pole.) When two discs are used, it takes three moves to go from the right side to the left side. This is because a larger disc is not allowed on a smaller disc. Here's how it's done: The smaller

Figure 2–3 *Tower of Hanoi Puzzle*

MATH MISCONCEPTIONS

disc gets placed on the middle pole. (That's the first move.) Then the larger disc gets placed on the left pole. (That's the second move.) Finally the smaller disc gets placed on top of the larger disc on the left pole. (That's the third move.) When three discs are used, it takes seven moves to go from one far peg to the other. Ask students whether they notice a pattern as they move the discs. They should also look for patterns in the numbers of moves, thus being able to predict how many moves it will take to move four, five, and six discs. (They may not be able to make these moves, but they will try enthusiastically.) Master-Mind® requires that students notice patterns that emerge from the clues given as one predicts which colors are hidden. Even games like chess, checkers, and tic-tac-toe involve noticing and mastering patterns of play in order to win. Keep a "games cart" in the classroom for older students to play when their class work is completed or during an indoor recess.

Questions to Ponder

1. Where in your academic curriculum could you introduce and reinforce patterns?

2. How do you reinforce repeating and growing patterns with your students?

Meaning of Equals

A class of second graders is trying to complete two number sentences recorded in a nontraditional way: 14 = ___ + 7 and ___ = 6 + 9. The students are puzzled. "I don't get it!" "Why are the answers in the front?" "They're backward. Maybe Ms. Morgan got mixed up."

Asked about the task, students offer reasons the task is so hard: "The 14 should be on the other side." "You can't do it this way. It's the wrong way to do the problem." "Maybe I can write the answer first. I'm not sure." "Why is the equals sign at the front?"

Later, a student records a 21 in the blank in the first problem, explaining, "Well, there's a plus sign and that means I have to add. Fourteen and 7 is 21." Another student extends the second number sentence this way: ___ = 6 + 9 = 15. She explains that she added 6 + 9 to get 15. Asked what should go on the line to the left of the original equals sign, she eventually replies, "Thirty. I think the plus means to add up all the numbers."

Ms. Morgan raises another question. What if the unknown appears like this: 8 + 3 = ___ + 4? What number will make the equation true?

Students seem confused. There is silence until a few students insist the number in the blank space should be 11, perhaps viewing the equals sign as a signal to add the numbers before it (and ignoring the 4 in the expression on the right).

Identifying the Error Pattern

The way these number sentences were written clearly presented difficulty for these students. Seeing the equals sign placed this way contradicted their earlier experiences. Their doubts revealed a limited understanding of the equals sign as a representation of equality—that what is on the left side of the equals sign must balance with what is on the right side.

In the number sentence $14 = \_\_ + 7$, the student's solution of 21 revealed that he had misinterpreted earlier patterns to mean that two numbers and a plus sign get added. This is a common problem for students who have never seen an expression configured like this. They overgeneralize their limited understanding of addition and subtraction. Similarly, $3 = \_\_ - 2$ might produce an equation like this, $3 = 1 - 2$. There are two numbers and a minus sign, so the lesser number is subtracted from the greater number.

The student who extended her number sentence so it read $\_\_ = 6 + 9 = 15$ also saw two numbers and a plus sign. Her placement of 15 at the end made sense to her: it was a familiar format. Asked about the extra space, she ignored the first equals sign, added all the numbers together, and recorded 30 on the line. None of these students viewed the equals sign as a symbol indicating that a balanced relationship must exist between the expressions on either side.

What the Research Says

Teachers, curriculums, and many textbooks view arithmetic and algebra as distinct and different. As a result students are denied opportunities to connect arithmetic and algebra. This impedes their understanding of critical ideas such as equality, and they encounter difficulties in later grades. A nonmathematical sense of the equals sign is "one of the major stumbling blocks for students when they move from arithmetic to algebra" (Falkner, Levi, and Carpenter 1999). We need to be sure students understand that a balance must exist on either side of the equals sign—that it represents the relationship of equality.

Simply explaining the meaning of the equals sign is not as effective as providing activities that foster this understanding. "A concerted effort over an extended period of time is required to establish appropriate notions of equality" (Falkner, Levi, and Carpenter 1999, 233). This idea should be introduced in kindergarten using a balance scale.

◫ *Ideas for Instruction*

▶ Develop an understanding of the part-whole relationship. "The ability to think about a number in terms of its parts is a major milestone in the development of number" (Van de Walle and Lovin 2006). Opportunities to develop this understanding enable students to develop fluency with numbers, the foundation for their later work with addition, subtraction, and algebraic thinking. For example, a student with a good understanding of this relationship can fluently state combinations for 8 as 1 and 7, 2 and 6, 3 and 5, 4 and 4, 5 and 3, 6 and 2, and 7 and 1, as well as 0 and 8 and 8 and 0. (And some can include combinations consisting of more than two parts, such as 2 and 3 and 3 or 4 and 3 and 1.)

■ Many kindergarten and first-grade teachers use Shake and Spill to show number components. Students shake and spill a designated number of bicolored (such as red and yellow) counters and record the results. For example, if the designated number is 7, combinations are recorded as 3 red and 4 yellow, 2 red and 5 yellow, or 1 red and 6 yellow. (This could be also be done on a themed mat with counters that fall inside or outside the picture.) (See Figure 2–4.)

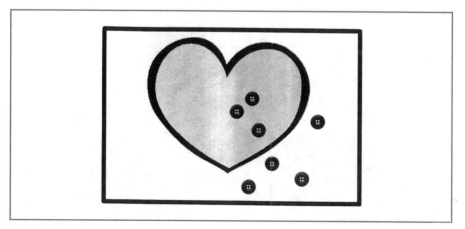

Figure 2–4 *One Way to Make 7*

■ A similar activity for second graders is to have them represent two-digit numbers with sticks of ten connecting cubes and single cubes. For example, 34 is represented as 3 tens and 4 ones, 2 tens and 14 ones, 1 ten and 24 ones, and 34 ones (also see the place value discussion on pages 14–20). These kinds of activities not only deepen children's understanding of the part-whole concept, they also support their ability to think flexibly about number, skills that are important when students determine the unknown in a variety of number sentences.

▶ Have students, in pairs, use a balance scale and weighted teddy bear counters to explore equality. For example, 1 mama bear is equal in weight to 2 baby bears or 1M = 2B. Also, 1P = 1M + 1B, or 1P = 3B. Bear-family counters (papa, mama, and baby, with proportional weights of 12, 8, and 4 grams) in four colors (red, green, blue, and yellow) can be purchased from most educational supply catalogs. Activity sheets are included in *Activities to Undo Math Misconceptions, Grades PreK–2*, pages 44–45.

▶ Promote an understanding of equality by using a number balance (available in educational supply catalogs), a T-shaped balance with twenty pegs (ten on each

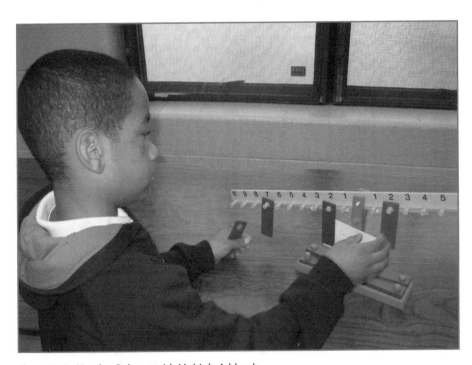

Figure 2–5 *Number Balance with Multiple Addends*

side of the fulcrum), which hold ten one-gram weights. These weights are placed on pegs to the left and right of the fulcrum to create equalities as well as inequalities (see Figure 2–5).

For example, if a student places a weight on peg 8 to the left of the fulcrum, the right side can now be balanced by placing weights on pegs 1, 2, and 5 (many other combinations are possible). Once students are familiar with how the balance works, they can create equations that represent the weights on the balance. In the example above, $8 = 1 + 2 + 5$ would be recorded.

▶ Anticipate students' overgeneralization about the equals sign by varying how equations are presented. Don't always place the unknown on the right of the equals sign—let them see it on the left as well (for example, ___ $= 6 + 9$). Discuss how the number chosen to fill in an unknown makes the number sentence *true*. Use reasoning to prove the sense of the equation.

▶ Routinely ask, "Is this true?" Take a number sentence students already know, such as $6 + 4 = 10$, and ask, "Is this true?" Expect them to explain how they know the equation is true (or correct). Other examples include:

$12 = 12$	$2 + 4 = 1 + 5$	$25 = 15 + 10$	$1 + 4 = 7 - 2$
$12 + 2 = 2 + 12$	$6 - 0 = 6$	$18 = 22 - 4$	$12 - 5 = 7 + 5$

Use larger numbers with students in intermediate grades.

▶ Use Cuisenaire® Rods to support students' development of equality. In a set of Cuisenaire® Rods, there are ten different-color rods that are also different sizes. The smallest rod is a white rod, which can be assigned the value of 1. The orange rod is ten times as long as a white rod. Once students have had time to explore the rods and become familiar with their values, ask them to represent the orange rod in a variety of ways using the remaining rods and their assigned values. For example, an orange rod can be represented as one blue rod (9) and one white rod (1). This can be recorded as $10 = 9 + 1$ (see Figure 2–6). Students are representing a number in a variety of ways, and these understandings support them when they think about unknowns in equations as well as strengthen their number sense. (A recording sheet for this activity is included in *Activities to Undo Math Misconceptions, Grades 3–5*.)

▶ Introduce the activity Mystery Number Squares (see *Activities to Undo Math Misconceptions, Grades PreK–2*, page 46 and *Activities to Undo Math Misconceptions, Grades 3–5*, page 50), in which students place numbered squares in boxes

Name _____ Date _____

Representing 10

How many different ways can the orange rod be represented? Record your work below.

The first one is done for you!

Orange rod = 10 white rods
10 = 1 + 1 + 1 + 1 + 1 + 1 + 1 + 1 + 1 + 1

Try more on the back!

Figure 2–6 *Representing 10 Activity*

to create balanced equations. Placing the equals signs in nontraditional ways helps students focus on the relationship of equality.

Questions to Ponder

1. "Is it true?" is one strategy you can use to help your students understand the meaning of the equals sign. Create several examples of number sentences your students could discuss.

2. What other instructional experiences can you introduce that will help your students better understand that the equals sign represents the relationship of equality?

Mrs. Sullivan begins the lesson by showing her fourth graders how to construct a single-span bridge using toothpicks. She builds a model on the overhead projector and asks the class the number of toothpicks used. Then she builds models of a two-span and three-span bridge, again recording the number of toothpicks used below each one (see Figures 2–7a and b).

The class organizes the data on a table (see Figure 2–7b).

Then Mrs. Sullivan asks the students to find the number of toothpicks needed to build a ten-span bridge. The classroom buzzes with activity. Large pieces of construction paper, placed strategically about the room, are surrounded by small groups of children equipped with a box of 250 toothpicks, a bottle of glue, and markers. Student groups are busy placing toothpicks and discussing the number of toothpicks needed for the next-largest bridge. Mrs. Sullivan moves from group to group, listening to their reasoning as they work.

"Let's finish the chart up to 5 and then just double the answer," Bella announces.

"Why would we do that?"

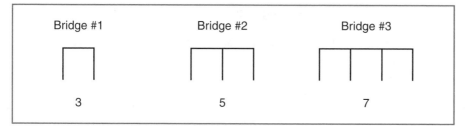

Figure 2–7a *Bridge Pattern*

Figure 2–7b *Table of Bridge Data*

Number of Toothpicks Needed to Build Bridges

Bridge Spans	1	2	3	4	5
Number of Toothpicks Needed	3	5	7		

"Because 10 is 5 doubled, so if we find the answer for 5, we could just double it to get the answer for 10."

Sam counts out more toothpicks as Bella and Tyson place them on the paper to form the four-span and five-span bridges.

"Okay, the five-span bridge needs 11 toothpicks. Eleven times 2 is 22. So a ten-span bridge will take 22 toothpicks, right?"

"Yep, that's it," responds Bella excitedly.

In another group Connor and Lodeon are assembling each successively larger bridge and counting toothpicks. Shelby explains, "We are going to tape a piece of paper on to this end so we can make the table longer. We will just keep going with the patterns until we get to 10."

"I know this one [pointing to the eight-span bridge] is going to be 17," Lodeon announces.

Mrs. Sullivan asks, "How do you know?"

"Because we are counting by twos. The last one was 15, so this one will be 17. That means that the ten-span bridge will need 21 toothpicks. I counted 18, 19 [for nine spans] and then 20, 21 [for ten spans]."

"Could you figure out how many toothpicks you'd need for a hundred-span bridge?"

The group gasps at the mere suggestion of such a large number.

"Oh my, we would need a whole lot more paper and tons more toothpicks," says Connor, his eyes wide.

"I think there is a faster way. We could just count by twos starting with the 3 until we get to 100," suggests Shelby.

"That would still take a long time," worries Connor.

Before she moves on, Mrs. Sullivan challenges the group to talk more about their strategy and come up with a plan for the hundred-span bridge.

Tung's group has taken still a different approach. They've left their toothpicks in the box and annotated their chart with a formula (see Figure 2–8).

"Tell me about your strategy," Mrs. Sullivan says.

Figure 2–8 *Tung's Group Work*

Bridge Spans	1	2	3	4	5
Number of Toothpicks Needed	3	5	7		

$\widehat{}$ 10

$$7 \quad 2 - 1L$$
$$x - 1$$

"We counted and it was 7 more steps to get from 3 to 10. We know each step is 2 more toothpicks, so 7 times 2 equals 14. It will take 14 toothpicks to make a ten-span bridge," explains Ruben.

Identifying the Error Pattern

Bella's group decided to find the total toothpicks for the five-span bridge and double that value for the ten-span bridge. This generated an answer of 22, 1 larger than the correct answer. While the group correctly considered the relationship between 5 and 10, they did not consider the nature of the function as it related to the number of toothpicks. The group could have tested their conjecture by doubling some of the previous values from the table. For example, if they had taken the number of toothpicks for a two-span bridge (5) and doubled it (10) and then looked on the chart at the number needed for a four-span bridge, they would have noticed it was 9, not 10. They also failed to notice that while all the values (number of toothpicks needed) were odd, their response was an even number.

Shelby's group extended the pattern correctly, having recognized the recursive relationships for the two variables; the number of spans increases by 1 and the number of toothpicks needed increases by 2. However, they did not see the functional relationship between the two variables: bridge span times 2 plus 1 equals the number of toothpicks ($y = 2x + 1$).

Tung's group abandoned the toothpicks and went right to work applying an equation to solve this problem. They correctly counted the number of remaining steps and multiplied by 2 to reflect the recursive pattern for the number of toothpicks (7 steps times 2 toothpicks equals 14 toothpicks). However, they failed to add to that total the number of toothpicks used for the three-span bridge, which was where they started counting the steps. If they had added 7 to their answer of 14, they would have arrived at the correct answer of 21 toothpicks.

Mrs. Sullivan's students were well versed in recognizing the growing patterns for each variable, an important step in helping students see functional relationships. All of her students were empowered to solve this problem and apply strategies based on their current level of understanding. They were now ready for intervention designed to take their conceptual knowledge one step further.

▋▋ *What the Research Says*

The National Council of Teachers of Mathematics (NCTM) defines two specific expectations for students in grades 3 through 5 with regard to understanding patterns, relations, and functions. They must be able to:

▶ Describe, extend, and make generalizations about geometric and numeric patterns.

▶ Represent and analyze patterns and functions using words, tables, and graphs.

The inclusion of "words, tables, and graphs" emphasizes the notion that students need experiences with multiple representations of functional patterns. Each representation offers a different "view" of the function. "It is important to see that each representation is a way of looking at the function, yet each provides a different way of looking at or thinking about the function" (Van de Walle 2007). One student may deduce the relationship between two variables from a table, another may need to construct the pattern using manipulative materials in order for the function to be revealed, and still another may need to "talk it out" while creating an equation to represent a function. Teachers must expose students to a variety of methods of communicating functional relationships, including physical models, pictorial models, symbolic models, and verbal models. Providing varied representations gives students a comprehensive look at this component of algebraic thinking, and this fact needs to be considered when planning instruction, whether it be an introductory lesson, a reteaching session, or an intervention.

▋▋ *Ideas for Instruction*

▶ Provide opportunities for students to explore growing patterns. Growing patterns are precursors to functional relationships (in a functional relationship, any step can be determined by the step number, without calculating all the steps in between). Students observe the step-by-step progression of a recursive pattern and continue the sequence.

▶ Choose or create a meaningful context—a scenario to which students can relate—for functional relationships. Examples include:

- Money spent on candy
- Ingredients needed for a recipe
- Blocks linked to build towers
- Time required to run a relay race
- Fuel needed for a vacation

▶ Allow students to construct physical models of functional relationships using tiles, toothpicks, connecting cubes, or a variety of other hands-on materials. The act of placing toothpicks in a specified pattern or connecting cubes in a sequence can provide insight into the relationship between the two variables.

▶ Compare physical models with pictorial or symbolic representations. For example, consider the growing pattern of triangles in Figure 2–9.

Regardless of the representation, the function remains the same. If asked to find the perimeter of the triangles in step 25, some students may choose to extend the table and continue the growing pattern for the steps and the corresponding perimeter. Others may prefer to use pattern blocks and physically construct a few steps until the function is revealed. This comparison may better enable students to identify a symbolic representation of the functional relationship based on the step number. If n equals the step number, then $n + 2$ equals the perimeter, so step 25 would have a perimeter of 27 units.

▶ Model the language of the dependent relationship and encourage students to describe the relationship. Examples include:

- *The amount of money I spend depends on how much candy I buy.*

Figure 2–9 *Growing Patterns with Triangles*

Step #	Step 1	Step 2	Step 3	Step 4	Step 5
Representation	△	▽	△▽	△▽△	△▽△▽
Perimeter	**3 units**	**4 units**	**5 units**	**6 units**	**7 units**

- *The number of cups of flour needed is determined by the number of pancakes we would like to make.*
- *The height of the tower affects the number of blocks linked.*
- *The time required to complete the race is a function of the distance of the race.*
- *The amount of fuel we use is directly related to the miles traveled.*

▶ Reinforce number sense through estimation. When students are able to articulate their intuitive understanding of the relationship, they may estimate and solve the function simultaneously. Estimation may help a student more readily recognize an error. (For example, estimation might have helped Tung's group when they failed to add the seven toothpicks from the previous bridge.)

▶ Have students graph the relationships revealed in a function. This provides a visual picture as they learn about rates of change.

▪▪ Questions to Ponder

1. What varied representations can be used to illustrate a functional relationship?

2. Using the sequence of triangles in the example above, what questions can you pose to students to assess their current level of understanding?

═ Interpreting Variables

Diane Parker assumes her fifth graders will be able to figure out the variables in an addition equation. After all, they've been solving multidigit expressions since second grade. So she gives them a very simple open-ended exercise. Drawing four squares, two over two, she asks, "If you had the digits 1, 2, 3, and 4, how would you place them in these squares so that you'd end up with the largest possible sum?" (See Figure 2–10.)

Working with a partner, the students brainstorm their answer. Dominic says confidently, "First we put the 4 in the tens place of the first number and the 3 in the ones place. Then we put the 2 in the tens place of the second number and the 1 in the ones place. That makes 43 plus 21. The sum is 64."

Surprised, Ms. Parker asks whether everyone has the same answer. Patricia says that she and her partner have produced a larger sum. Ms. Parker asks

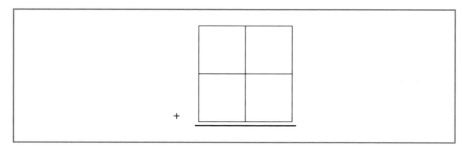

Figure 2–10 *Template for Largest Sum*

them where they placed the digits and how they knew it would give them the highest possible sum.

"We put the two biggest numbers in the tens place since that would already give us 70. Then it didn't really matter where we put the 2 and the 1. Thirty-two plus 41 equals 73. And 31 plus 42 also equals 73," Patricia explains.

Ms. Parker asks whether anyone has a different way to arrange the digits to create a sum greater than 73. No one raises a hand. She then asks whether everyone has heard and understood what Patricia has said. Most of the students nod their head, but several look confused. So Ms. Parker asks Meghan to rephrase Patricia's answer.

A bit hesitantly, Ms. Parker then gives the students the same four squares and the same four digits and asks them to place these in the correct places to create the greatest difference possible. As she walks around the room she hears students talking about what the word *difference* means. So she interrupts their work and asks what operation they would use if they were looking for the difference between two numbers. Anthony says they need to subtract.

Again circulating through the room, Ms. Parker sees that the strategy being used most often is guess and check. Only a few students seem to know that for the difference to be the greatest there needs to be a 4 in the tens place of the minuend and a 1 in the tens place of the subtrahend.

After sufficient time, Ms. Parker asks Jessica to share how she and Timothy got their answer. Jessica explains that they tried a lot of different configurations before getting 43 − 12 = 31. Ms. Parker asks whether this is the answer others have gotten and most students say yes. Then she asks whether everyone used the guess-and-check strategy to get the answer—and is relieved when several children say they used Patricia's strategy from before to set up the problem.

Algebra Challenge

Use the digits 0, 1, 2, 3, 4, 5, 6, 7, 8, or 9 to make the equation below true. A letter must always represent the same digit (for example, if you decide that A = 3, every A must equal 3).

```
  M A N
+ F A N
—————
  M E L T
```

There are many correct answers for this challenge. Try to get at least one.

Figure 2–11 *Algebra Challenge*

"This time," Jonathan says, "you have to have the highest number in the tens place in the top number and the smallest number in the tens place in the bottom number. Then you'd get thirty-something. In the ones place, the 3 goes on top and the 2 goes on the bottom."

Hoping everyone has heard and understood this, Ms. Parker gives them the challenge for the day (see Figure 2–11).

Only a few students begin talking about how to solve this puzzler. Most seem to think it's a foreign language they don't understand.

▪▪ *Identifying the Error Pattern*

These students' inability to decipher the problem isn't really an error pattern. It's more a misconception about the nature of variables and how they can be used. Variables can be used in three different contexts: as unknowns, as changing quantities, and in generalizations of patterns (NCTM 2000, 39). Young students often see a box replacing an addend in an open addition equation. They realize that the box represents some quantity and it's their job to figure out the numeral that replaces the box. Students also see variables whenever they use a formula (that is, to find the area of a rectangle, they use the formula $l \times w$). And variables are also used in elementary classrooms to show how height changes based on age.

Perhaps these fifth graders were confused because they'd rarely seen a letter representing a digit in an equation. The idea that a variable can stand for any single-digit whole number might be a concept that only a few of these students had encountered and most did not understand. Juxtaposing arithmetic and algebra may be very confusing to students who have never "played" with numbers before.

What the Research Says

"Students may have difficulty if they view algebra as generalized arithmetic. Arithmetic and algebra use the same symbols and signs but interpret them differently" (Billstein, Libeskind, and Lott 2007, 40). This can be very confusing to students, particularly if their arithmetic concepts and skills are weak.

"Many students think all variables are letters that stand for numbers. Yet the values a variable takes are not always numbers, even in high school mathematics" (Usiskin 1988, 10). In middle school a variable can be used to represent identifying points on polygons. In high school logic, p and q are used to stand for propositions. The idea that a letter can replace only a numeral is a misconception many students have—one that is supported by educators who view problems like $5 + x = 12$ as algebra but $5 + \square = 12$ as arithmetic.

In the elementary grades letters appear in arithmetic as abbreviations. The letter m is used to represent the word *meter*. It's no wonder that when students see $4m$ they are thinking about four meters rather than four times the variable m. And can you imagine student's confusion when they see $p = 2l + 2w$? How does a teacher get around this when it's logical for p to stand for *perimeter*, l for length, and w for *width*? A study conducted in the United Kingdom from 1980 to 1983 found that students frequently questioned whether a letter was used to represent some numerical value or an abbreviation for a word (Booth 1984, 20–32). And even when students realize that a letter is being used to replace a numerical value, many still assume this is a unique value rather than a general number (Kuchemann 1981).

Ideas for Instruction

Early childhood and elementary school students need to be exposed to variables in a number of different ways:

▶ Use variables as labels and abbreviations. Teachers often ask young children to identify the elements in a repeating pattern with letters of the alphabet. A pattern made with alternating circles and squares can be called an AB pattern just as easily as it can be named by the shapes within it or the colors of these shapes. Done intentionally, this introduces students to the way that letters can be used in mathematics. In later grades there is no reason at all that polygons cannot be labeled with letters identifying each vertex. It is also sensible to have fifth graders who are learning about angles in geometry identify these angles with letters.

▶ Have students look for places where a letter is used to represent some word. You can also create a series of these "mathematical equations" around a theme and ask students to solve them. The following examples all relate to time:
7 = D. in a W.

12 = M. in a Y.

4 = S. in a Y.

31 = D. in J., M., M., J., A., O., and D.

60 = M. in an H.

60 = S. in a M.

24 = H. in a D.

100 = Y. in a C.

> Answers: 7 = Days in a Week; 12 = Months in a Year; 4 = Seasons in a Year; 31 = Days in January, March, May, July, August, October, and December; 60 = Minutes in an Hour; 60 = Seconds in a Minute; 24 = Hours in a Day; 100 = Years in a Century.

▶ Point out how letters are used in the formulas you are teaching. Even as early as third grade children are learning to use formulas to find the area and perimeter of polygons. Unfortunately, many just memorize the formula and don't understand what the letters refer to. If using a variable in this manner is to make sense to students, the formula should be the last thing they learn as they find area and perimeter. Begin by posing a problem that students can understand—fencing in a pet or making a garden that deer and rabbits cannot get to. Or perhaps you want to have an 18-square-foot garden. Asking students to figure out all the different shapes your garden could have is a good way for them to see the relationship between area and spatial arrangement. Once they decide on the best shape for the garden, have them figure out how much fencing you'll need so that deer and rabbits don't eat all the plants. It's not difficult for third graders to see that a garden plot that is 3 feet by 6 feet has an area of 18 square feet (obtained by multiplying the length of the garden by its width). And the amount of fencing in feet is found by taking both lengths and both widths and adding them together. In this way, students derive the formula on their own and it's just a matter of having them replace the words with the initials that begin each word.

▶ Begin replacing the "box" in an arithmetic equation with a letter as soon as students recognize the difference between letters and numerals. This may seem like a recipe for trouble, but second graders realize that if a number is missing from an equation they have to do something to figure out what that number is. A second-grade teacher can say, "Last year you were solving to find the number that made this equation true. Instead of using a box to hold the place of the number could we use a letter instead? What letter might be good to use until we figure out the number?" Most students get the idea that n, for number, would be a good letter to use. Start with simple equations: $n + 6 = 9$; $7 - n = 4$; $8 = 5 + n$; $5 = n - 2$. Approaching these equations as a puzzle creates a mystique different from solving straightforward expressions. Many students like the idea of being a detective trying to solve for n. Students capable of finding the missing digit in two-digit numbers are ready for this kind of problem: $3\_ + 5\_ = \_7$. There are lots of right answers: $31 + 56 = 87$, $32 + 55 = 87$, $33 + 54 = 87$, $34 + 53 = 87$, and so on. You can also ask students to find all the possible solutions. Again, once students are comfortable finding a digit to replace the blank space, a letter can be put in the same spot. Their strategies will be the same, but they'll be solving for a letter instead of a blank space. If the letter is a capital rather than a lowercase letter, there should be less of a problem.

▦ *Questions to Ponder*

1. What sorts of manipulative materials could you use to help young students understand how to solve for a missing number?

2. Once formulas have been introduced into the curriculum, how can you help students see the different uses for variables?

⬛ **Algebraic Representations**

The school year is nearing the winter holidays. Although Ms. Burton hasn't officially introduced ideas of addition and subtraction to her first graders, they have been working on ways to represent story problems with materials and drawings.

Several students are even attempting to write (using invented spelling) about what they've done to get their answers. She decides to give them a story problem connected to some of the holiday songs they have been learning:

> Santa decided it was too cold for his reindeer. He asked his elves to knit booties to keep the reindeer's hooves warm. Not wanting Rudolf to be left out, Santa told his elves to knit booties for all 9 of his reindeer. How many booties will the elves need to knit?

After reading this story to the students Ms. Burton asks them if they know what booties are. Samuel shares that his baby sister wears booties on her feet because she doesn't wear shoes yet. Ms. Burton says that the booties keep Sam's baby sister's feet warm the same way that Santa wants to keep his reindeer's hooves warm.

Then Ms. Burton says, "I wonder how many legs each reindeer has?" Many students raise their hand. She calls on Tommy. As Tommy answers, Ms. Burton writes on her whiteboard that reindeer have 4 legs and that on each leg there is a hoof. "Just like people have feet at the bottom of their legs, reindeer have hooves at the bottom of their legs."

Next Ms. Burton tells the children they can work alone or with a partner and that they can draw pictures, use words, use numbers, and even use counters to help them figure out the answer to this story problem. Then she reads it one more time.

While the students work on the problem, Ms. Burton walks around the room. She isn't sure whether this story is too challenging, given the large number of reindeer and the even larger number of booties that will be required. Still, she's curious to see what they can do.

Alicia is working with Danielle. The girls are using connecting cubes and have several sticks of 4 cubes on their desks. Ms. Burton asks them to explain what they are doing, and Danielle speaks up. "These are the reindeer," she says, pointing to the sticks of 4 cubes.

"Is each cube in a stick a reindeer, or is the stick of cubes the reindeer?" Ms. Burton asks. The girls look at each other but say nothing. "What does this whole stick represent?" Ms. Burton asks.

"It's the reindeer," Alicia responds.

"So if the stick is the whole reindeer, what does each cube represent?"

"It's the reindeer," Danielle repeats.

Ms. Burton tries a different question. "How did you decide that you'd put 4 cubes into each of these sticks?"

"Reindeer have 4 legs," Danielle says.

"So does each of the cubes represent the legs of each reindeer?" The look on the girls' faces makes clear they aren't sure what they are doing or why. "Keep working on this," Ms. Burton tells them. "We'll be talking about the strategies that everyone is using in a little while."

She walks over to Anthony, who is working alone. On a sheet of paper he's drawn several rows with 4 Xs in each row. "Tell me what you're doing to solve this story problem," Ms. Burton says.

"See, each of these Xs is the hoof of a reindeer. Reindeer have 4 legs; so they have 4 hooves. I'm making all of the reindeer."

Ms. Burton wants to be sure Anthony knows that an entire row of Xs represents one reindeer but doesn't want to confuse him. After thinking a minute she says, "Tell me how you decided to put these Xs into rows like this."

"If I just made a lot of Xs I wouldn't be able to figure out how many reindeer there are. Every one of these [pointing to the rows] stands for a reindeer."

"So how will you figure out how many booties the elves need to knit?"

"I'll just count them."

"What will you be counting?"

"The Xs, because they're for the feet," Anthony says, smiling.

Ms. Burton is pleased, but as she walks around the room, asking different students questions about what they are modeling, drawing, or writing, she notices that many aren't sure whether they should be drawing reindeer or legs/hooves. And some of the students drawing hooves (or representations of them) tell her these are the reindeer.

Identifying the Error Pattern

Assuming that a seemingly correct representation ensures a student's complete understanding of a quantitative relationship can be misleading. Many educators think that simply using a manipulative, a drawing, or an equation enables students to understand how to solve a problem successfully. But if students do not fully understand the relationship involved in a given quantitative situation, the representation they are using will not make sense to them.

In Ms. Burton's classroom, Alicia and Danielle were using sticks of cubes to work through the problem. They initially seemed to understand how to go about solving it. But when Ms. Burton continued to ask questions about what they were doing, it became evident they were confused. Although Alicia and Danielle knew there were 4 legs on a reindeer, they still had not made the connection about how those legs related to the number of booties each reindeer needed. They probably had not yet learned how to organize their thoughts about a quantitative situation, so explaining their representation was difficult. The use of the sticks of cubes made solving the problem even more difficult.

The good news is that giving children numerous opportunities to reflect or talk about a problem helps them choose meaningful representations. This talk needs to occur not only before problem solving begins but during and afterward as well. When students describe their own problem-solving strategies and listen to how classmates have solved a problem, they begin to make sense of how different representations can make sense in a variety of mathematical situations. Allowing students to reflect on a problem-solving task and how it can be represented in different ways helps them learn to organize their thinking and use representations more effectively.

What the Research Says

The following recommendations related to representation, issued by the National Council of Teachers of Mathematics (NCTM), will help you plan and present instructional lessons and activities to develop your students' understanding of mathematics.

Instructional programs from prekindergarten though grade 12 should enable all students to:

- create and use representations to organize, record, and communicate mathematical ideas

- select, apply, and translate [from] among mathematical representations to solve problems

- use representations to model and interpret physical, social, and mathematical phenomena

Young students use a variety of manipulatives to represent quantitative relationships and mathematical ideas, modeling many different mathematical situations that involve smaller quantities. However, when quantities become larger and more complex, manipulatives become unmanageable and are an inefficient way to represent how to solve a problem. Students then realize that a pictorial or graphic representation will serve them better, and this kind of representation becomes more sophisticated in later school years.

It is critical that students have numerous opportunities to represent problem solving using concrete and pictorial representations before using abstract representations. Ennis and Witeck (2007) propose that using abstract representations such as numbers and equations requires a deep understanding of a topic. Moving students too quickly to abstract representations encourages them to perform certain procedures by rote without understanding why these procedures work or what they mean. "However, we would be negligent as well if we did not help students make the connection between ideas and equations and see how equations can help us solve problems and visualize ideas" (Ennis and Witeck 2007).

We've discussed three stages of representations that students use to represent quantitative relationships and other mathematical ideas. It's important that we allow students to choose the representation that enables them to show their thinking about how to solve a problem. For example, some students may choose to represent their thinking using a drawing, while others are more comfortable with manipulatives. Choosing from a variety of representations helps students understand that some representations are more useful than others when solving a particular problem.

But simply telling students how to use a manipulative step by step to solve a specific problem doesn't help them. The representation becomes a rote procedure rather than an aid to help them make sense of a problem. Little understanding is being developed when a representation is used in a procedural way (Van de Walle and Lovin 2006). By encouraging our students to use a representation in a way that makes sense to them, we allow them to think and reflect about the mathematical idea involved in solving the problem.

Ideas for Instruction

▶ Provide opportunities for students to explore, and then talk about, a variety of manipulatives. Model the correct vocabulary specific to each manipulative. Plan lessons in which students use these manipulatives.

▶ Encourage students to use multiple representations. Create and model an environment in which all explanations and representations are honored and respected.

▶ Allow students to select different representations to use in solving any problem. It is critical that students choose and use representations that are meaningful to them (NCTM 2000). Knowing which type of representation is useful in which situation is an important milestone in mathematical understanding and reasoning.

▶ Ask students to explain and show how they are thinking during and following a problem-solving task. If students are having difficulty, support them by the type of questions you ask. Hearing how others use representations to show how they are thinking about a mathematical idea helps students consider other perspectives. Communicating thinking requires students to reflect on their problem solving and reasoning; listening to students' explanations enables teachers to determine what students know and can do at any point in time.

▶ Provide opportunities for students to solve many open-ended tasks with a representation they have chosen. Follow these problem-solving tasks with classroom discussions. These representations can also be shared with parents to communicate their child's understanding of the mathematical concepts and skills being taught.

▶ Model for students how to record their way of solving a problem using numbers. Be sure to record a student's method both horizontally and vertically.

▶ When students use a representation, ask probing questions to determine whether they understand their representation and how to use it to solve the problem effectively.

▶ Use literature to engage students in open-ended problem solving and ask them to represent their solutions in a representation that makes sense to them. Here are two examples:

  ■ *Rooster's Off to See the World*, by Eric Carle. On a venture to see the world, a rooster is joined by two cats, then three frogs, then four turtles, and finally five fish. Once the story has been read, ask primary students to figure out how many animals there are in all and to show how they know in a representation. Expect students to describe and explain their representations.

  ■ *Tiger Math*, by Ann Whitehead Nagda and Cindy Bickel. The growth of a Siberian tiger cub is chronicled with a series of different types of graphs. These graphical representations are a springboard for showing students how to interpret mathematical relationships in many forms.

▟ Questions to Ponder

1. Why is it important to model many ways to use representations? Why is it important for students to explain and show how they used a representation to communicate their thinking about how to solve a problem?

2. Think about the types of representations your students are now using. Do they use the same representation for every problem? Do they choose one representation over another one because it is more efficient in helping them think about the task?

Geometry

Geometry is best explored actively, using tools and mathematics materials to construct conceptual knowledge. Hands-on experiences are instrumental in developing strong reasoning skills and the ability to solve increasingly complex geometric problems through visualization and spatial reasoning. Coordinate geometry is also important. Students must be able to represent location, direction, and distance. Another key expectation for intermediate students is the ability to apply transformations and use symmetry to analyze situations. The ability to move flexibly between two-dimensional representations and three-dimensional figures is best enhanced through experience.

 Categorizing Two-Dimensional Shapes

Mr. Norwitz's fifth graders are solving a geometry problem. Groups of students (four to a table) have a piece of paper on which ten quadrilaterals are drawn. They have rulers they can use if they want to. Working together, they are identifying all the parallelograms, rhombuses, rectangles, trapezoids, and squares and recording them (using the letter inside each quadrilateral) on their worksheet (see Figure 3–1).

They know that some shapes can belong to more than one category and therefore be in more than one column.

"Rectangles have to have two long sides and two short sides, so D and F are the only rectangles."

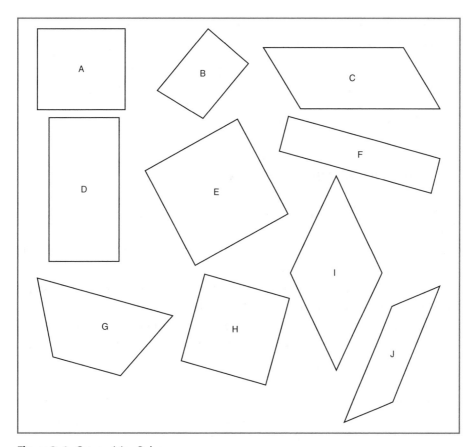

Figure 3–1 *Categorizing Polygons*

"There's only one trapezoid. It's G, but it's upside down, but we can still put it as a trapezoid."

"C and J are the only parallelograms."

"I think C is the only parallelogram. J is kind of sideways. It doesn't look like a parallelogram."

"I is a diamond, and there isn't a category for diamonds. Where does Mr. Norwitz want us to put I?"

"Well, there's no category for B either. What's the name of this shape?"

"A is probably a square and so is H. E is a sideways square or it could be a diamond."

"I think that E and I are both rhombuses."

"Mr. Norwitz said that some would be in more than one category, but none of our shapes are. We probably have things wrong."

"Are we supposed to have a category for every shape? Some of our shapes don't go in any of the columns on the chart!"

■■ *Identifying the Error Pattern*

What do you know about quadrilaterals? What makes a square a square, and what other ways can this shape be classified? How do we know when a shape is a parallelogram? Does the position of the shape impact its name? Did you think to yourself, *I'm not sure I know the correct answers to this problem*?

If you did, you're not alone. Many teachers tell us they never learned about shapes in the way they are being asked to teach them. They learned to identify shapes and then to define them. Lots of memorizing went on in a geometry unit but not lots of experiencing. So maybe before we discuss the challenges that students were having with the activity, we should look at the correct answers (see Figure 3–2).

These are not the answers these fifth graders were getting. If they'd been in prekindergarten through fourth-grade classrooms in which they made shapes with a variety of materials (pipe cleaners, Wiki sticks, geobands on geoboards) and identified them in the environment (in artwork, around the school and their homes, in activity books), wouldn't you expect students to be able to identify the properties that make up these shapes and use these properties to classify them? Then again, how many resource books label something a *diamond* when *rhombus* is the correct geometric term or call something an *oval* when it's really an *ellipse*? And where are the groupings of rectangles that include a square along with shapes that have two long sides and two shorter sides?

It's no wonder students identify shapes based on the limited images they've seen instead of defining them based on similar characteristics. A rectangle isn't just a quadrilateral with two long sides and two short sides; it's "a quadrilateral with four right angles. The opposite sides of a rectangle are congruent (of the same length) and are parallel" (Nichols and Schwartz 1993, 334). Therefore, a square is a special

Figure 3–2 *Answers to Categorizing Polygons*

Squares	Rectangles	Parallelograms	Rhombi	Trapezoids
E and H	A, D, E, F, H	A, C, D, E, F, H, I, J	E, H, I	B, G

rectangle. A square is a special parallelogram and rhombus, too. But students often learn to identify it only as a square and don't look at its properties that are characteristic of other figures as well. And if the only time students see trapezoids is when they are using pattern blocks, they could overgeneralize that all trapezoids look a certain way. Examples and nonexamples help students see the characteristics or properties of plane figures and allow them to move beyond a single example.

Does a shape's position have anything to do with its name? Nope! Yet there are still third graders who look at a rotated square and say, "Now it's a diamond!" If students do this in prekindergarten or kindergarten, it's excusable. But third graders should have encountered enough shapes, in a variety of sizes and positions, to know that the name stays the same.

■■ *What the Research Says*

Although the National Council of Teachers of Mathematics recommends that elementary curricula ask students to use "concrete models, drawings, and dynamic geometry software so that they can engage actively with geometric ideas" (NCTM 2000, 41), "research continues to indicate that, regrettably, little geometry is taught in the elementary grades, and that what is taught is often feeble in content and quality" (Fuys and Liebov 1993). The work of Pierre and Dina van Hiele (Van de Walle 2007, 400–404) has led the way for other mathematics researchers to better understand the different levels of geometric understanding and the variety of experiences that students need in order to move comfortably to the next level. We know that these levels have nothing to do with the grade students are in or with their age but rather relate to the experiences to which students are exposed and in which they participate.

Second graders being introduced to ideas of congruence for the first time should be given a variety of figures to look at, touch, and compare. Then they should be given nonexamples so they can see the difference between congruent figures and figures that aren't congruent. Finally, they should be given materials and told to make figures that are congruent to one another. In this way, they achieve the first level of knowledge—recognition.

Similarly, fifth graders being introduced to tessellations for the first time should be given a variety of examples to look at (including Escher artwork, perhaps), followed by nonexamples so that they can see the differences. Then they should be given materials to create their own tessellations.

In their research, Clements and Battista (1992) determined that primary-grade students were better able to recognize both two- and three-dimensional shapes when they handled models and were shown diagrams that included region or surface in addition to sides and edges. These researchers also stressed the importance of providing both examples and nonexamples of shapes, because nonexamples help students eliminate unimportant features and focus on relevant ones.

▪▪ *Ideas for Instruction*

Some ideas based on the van Hiele model of geometric thought:

▶ Go on a shape hunt: have prekindergarten through second-grade students identify shapes in their classroom, school, and home. Using "spy glasses" (see the accompanying CD and *Activities to Undo Math Misconceptions, Grades PreK–2*) students walk around the classroom or their neighborhood, find specific shapes, draw them, and indicate where they were found.

▶ Combine geometry with number concepts by having young students find different shapes on a worksheet (see Figure 3–3), color them different colors, determine how many of each shape there are, and record this number. This is another great way to identify shapes even when their sizes and positions are different.

▶ Use children's literature to introduce a mathematics lesson about shapes. Have children read math-related literature that includes accurate examples of plane fig-

Figure 3–3 *Find the Shapes*

ures. Be sure to find books that represent shapes in different sizes and in different positions. *Shapes, Shapes, Shapes*, by Tana Hoban (1986), features shapes students find in their environment. *The Greedy Triangle*, by Marilyn Burns (1994), introduces a variety of shapes, including polygons with more than six sides. It also reinforces where these shapes can be found. *Circus Shapes*, by Stuart Murphy (1998), shows students shapes at the circus (they are limited to rectangles, squares, circles, and triangles, which makes it ideal for very young children). Here are some other good books featuring shapes:

- Hewitt, Sally. 1996. *Take Off with Shapes*. Austin, TX: Raintree/Steck-Vaughn.
- Kassirer, Sue. 2001. *Math Fair Blues*. New York: The Kane Press.
- McMillan, Bruce. 1988. *Fire Engine Shapes*. New York: William Morrow.
- Onyefulu, Ifeonm. 2000. *A Triangle for Adaora: An African Book of Shapes*. New York: Penguin Putnam Books for Young Readers.
- Rogers, Paul. 1989. *The Shapes Game*. New York: Henry Holt.

▶ Develop "concept cards" of examples and nonexamples (see Figure 3–4).

▶ Develop *best examples*—"clear cases demonstrating the variation of the concept's attributes" (Tennyson, Youngers, and Suebsonthi 1983, 281)—for each two- and

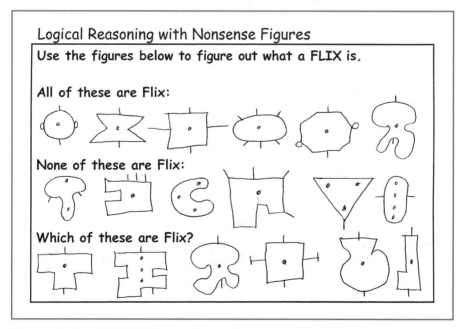

Figure 3–4 *What Do All "Flix" Have in Common?*

three-dimensional shape included in your curriculum. Ask students questions about these examples to determine whether they recognize the important properties of each. (This approach is more effective with third and fourth graders than having them look at examples and nonexamples.)

▶ Encourage students to describe, draw, model, identify, and classify shapes, as well as predict the results when shapes are combined and decomposed.

▶ Carefully select posters, math-related literature, and other commercial displays. Print materials may include only one variety of a shape (for example, show rectangles with only two long and two short sides) or incorrect shapes (ellipses that are incorrectly labeled as "ovals" and rhombuses that are labeled "diamonds").

▶ Allow students to create shapes from a variety of materials so they see regular as well as irregular shapes. (Geoboards and geobands are ideal for this sort of activity.)

▶ Have fourth and fifth graders use Venn diagrams to list common attributes of figures and classify them.

▶ Play games like "Guess My Shape," in which students draw a shape by following a series of clues.

▶ Incorporate other areas of geometry into activities with shapes (for example, create tessellations; transform shapes through rotations, translations, and reflections; combine shapes).

▦ *Questions to Ponder*

1. How can you use geometry activities in other content areas to help students see the purpose of understanding shapes and concepts surrounding shapes?

2. How does your knowledge about shapes impact your comfort level in teaching geometric ideas?

 ## Naming Three-Dimensional Figures

Margaret Thurman is an experienced kindergarten teacher. When she introduces three-dimensional solids, she creates a Museum of Solids using articles found at home so students can see how geometry plays a part in their lives.

She brings in oatmeal containers, soda and other cans, and even lipstick tubes so students can see the practical uses of cylinders. She displays birthday party hats, ice cream cones, and paper cups and borrows traffic cones from the local police station so she can show children real uses for cones. Rectangular prisms are easy to find since so many groceries are packaged in boxes of this shape. She collects balls of every size, from the tiniest marble to a basketball, so spheres are associated with things students play with all the time. She calls dice "number cubes," and whenever the children use cube-shaped blocks, she calls them wooden cubes.

She reads different pieces of math-related literature and has students come forward to point out the different solid figures that are mentioned in these books. She even has the children go on a scavenger hunt looking for different solids around the school.

When shown a row of various solid figures and asked to point to the cube, sphere, cone, rectangular prism, or cylinder, most students have no trouble doing so (even if they mispronounce *sphere*, calling these shapes *spears*).

Finally Ms. Thurman decides it's time to assess her students' knowledge of shapes. One by one she calls them to her table and shows them a wooden solid in each shape only to discover that many of these twenty-three students misidentify them. Six students don't even make an attempt at labeling a cylinder. See Figure 3–5 for the results of her assessment.

Figure 3–5 *Identifying Solid Figures*

cube	square 10	box 8	cube 5
sphere	circle 13	ball 6	sphere 4
cone	triangle 8	pointy thing 5	cone 10
rectangular prism	rectangle 14	box 7	rectangular prism 2
cylinder	roller 5	circle 10	cylinder 2

▪▪ *Identifying the Error Pattern*

If you are a primary teacher, the same thing has probably happened to you. Fortunately, by the time students get into the intermediate grades they have seen and used these three-dimensional solids so many times that they no longer name them incorrectly. But what causes young children to do this? It can't be that the names are too difficult to pronounce or remember. *Cube* and *cone* are single syllables and very easy to pronounce. And while *rectangular prism* may be complicated to say, this is insufficient cause for calling it a rectangle.

Several factors could have contributed to these students' difficulties. The first was that the unit of study was not undertaken until April. Students had already been looking at, identifying, and naming plane figures and most likely misidentifying some of these figures as two-dimensional when they were really solids. In looking for rectangles, students found the classroom door, filing cabinets, wooden building blocks, and the tops of desks. Although these figures are really all rectangular prisms, they had been praised for naming them rectangles. As students explored pattern blocks they referred to the orange block as a square and the green block as a triangle. But both of these blocks are prisms since they are able to be picked up and their sides are bounded by rectangles. Without realizing it, Ms. Thurman had taught students the incorrect names of many of the shapes she hoped they'd learn to correctly identify. When she finally introduced students to the correct names for several solid figures she had to undo learning that had taken place earlier in the year.

She also asked students to find and identify various shapes and showed them real uses for each, but she never familiarized them with the wooden solids she later used in her assessment. So the assessment task was different from most of the activities they had done during the preceding week. They could not apply what they had just learned to these "new" manipulatives they'd never used before.

▪▪ *What the Research\ Says*

Fuys and Liebov (1993) identify various misconceptions children have about geometric shapes. When they undergeneralize, students include irrelevant characteristics. When they overgeneralize, they omit key properties. Language-related misconceptions occur when they create their own inaccurate definitions (for example, that *diagonal* means *slanty*). The errors made by many of the students in Ms. Thurman's kindergarten class were overgeneralizations—they omitted the fact that the shapes were not plane figures but solid figures.

Clements and Battista (1992) found that children often form a geometric concept by noticing characteristics and then developing an "average representation" for any new example. Thus a student might think that spheres are circles if the focus is on the concept of "round" as a distinguishing feature. Also, research on visual discrimination by Hoffer (1977) indicates that young children sometimes lack the ability to distinguish similarities and differences between objects. This may account for a cube and a square being looked at as the same shape.

▪▪ *Ideas for Instruction*

▶ In prekindergarten mathematics programs, study solid figures before plane figures. Students see these three-dimensional figures in their environment and should know how to identify and name them.

▶ In the early fall, look at building blocks, table blocks, parquetry blocks, and pattern blocks and name them correctly.

▶ Label the shapes in the room. A globe can have the words *globe* and *sphere* alongside it. The door could display the term *rectangular prism* as well as the word *door*. These labels can be left in place for the duration of the year or until it's clear students can identify and name these solid figures. (The words can also be placed on a mathematics word wall alongside pictures representing the shape.)

▶ Introduce activities in which students find, color, name, and discuss the solid figures they need to learn about. This helps them generalize characteristics without being confused by size, color, and other unimportant attributes. Provide large, small, foam, wooden, and real-life examples of different solid figures. Then show students pictures of these figures (available in *Activities to Undo Math Misconceptions, Grades PreK–2,* page 62), have them identify the solid figure from the picture, and ask them to match it with the three-dimensional example. (Questions you might ask: *Is it okay for this to be a cone even though it's smaller than this cone? Can this still be a cylinder even though it's red? Would this still be called a sphere even if it was made out of plastic?*)

▶ Ask open-ended questions about solid figures so that children use mathematics vocabulary associated with attributes of these figures. For example, *what can you tell me about this shape?* is a better question to ask about a cube than *where do you see a square on this shape?* Even the youngest students can answer something when the question is open-ended. They may not talk about the faces, edges, or vertices of the shape, but they will use their own words to describe how it looks and feels. Then you can introduce the terminology they will encounter in the higher grades.

- If they have the necessary manual dexterity, have second and third graders fold plane diagrams (also called *nets*) of solid figures into the figures themselves. It is easier to explore the faces, edges, and vertices of a solid with a net than in an illustration. Doing so, students learn to distinguish between, for example, a triangle and a tetrahedron or a triangular prism.

- Using an overhead projector, show one face of a solid figure. Ask students to name this plane shape and guess the name of the solid figure from its shadow. This is an excellent way for students to begin thinking about the attributes that make up a solid figure. An accompanying worksheet could have pictures of solid figures in one column and pictures of plane figures in the other. Students draw a line from the solid figure to the matching plane figure. For example, show cubes, rectangular prisms that aren't cubes, cylinders, and cones on one side, and squares, rectangles that aren't squares, and circles on the other side. Students connect the cube to the square, the rectangular prism to the square or the rectangle, and the cylinder and cone to the circle.

- Place solid figures inside a bag and have students reach inside and, without looking, name the shape they are feeling. This activity helps them eliminate the distractions of color, size, and the names of the solid's faces.

- Give students a row of figures (five, say) in which only two are exactly the same. This builds student's visual discrimination and helps them focus on the concept of alike and different.

▨ *Questions to Ponder*

1. How might you reinforce the names and characteristics of solid figures while still introducing the names of plane figures?

2. How can you use what you know about teaching letter and word recognition to support teaching shape recognition?

▢ Navigating Coordinate Geometry

Blazer the dragon always elicits smiles and squeals of excitement from the students at Oak View Elementary. As the school mascot, he makes appearances at assemblies and special events. He is a cornerstone of the Oak View family.

Today Blazer is visiting Ms. Lawrence's math class and leading the students in a game of "Where's Blazer?" These third graders are learning to navigate coordinate grids, and Ms. Lawrence has decided this game will be a fun way for students to practice these skills.

A large coordinate grid is posted at the front of the room. A small version of the same grid showing where Blazer is hiding is ready to be projected onto the large grid. Once the class identifies his hiding spot by naming and marking the correct coordinates, the projector will be turned on to confirm his location. For this round, Blazer is hiding at point (7,4) (see Figure 3–6). The class begins naming points Blazer might be.

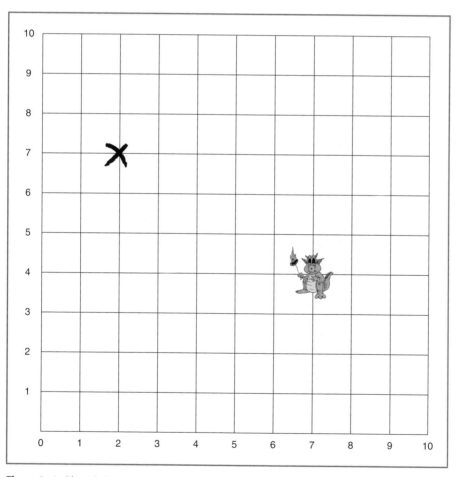

Figure 3–6 *Blazer's Game Board*

Maggie makes the first guess and puts an X on the coordinate point (2,7) on the posted grid. Blazer marks Maggie's guess on his game board and gives the clue "southeast" as the direction to travel next.

Noah places an X on the grid for his coordinate guess (3,3), but puts it in a space. Ms. Lawrence reminds Noah that they are naming points, not spaces. She takes a few moments to highlight the coordinates on the *x*- and *y*-axes and reminds the class they are the points of intersection, not the spaces between the points. Noah nods and moves his X to the correct point of intersection.

As students continue plotting points, the class gets closer to finding Blazer (see Figure 3–7). Selvin guesses (5,4) but places his X on the grid at (4,5). Dani's hand is at once in the air. She goes to the large grid and helps Selvin decide whether he wants (5,4) or (4,5). He settles on (5,4) and moved his X to that point. On the

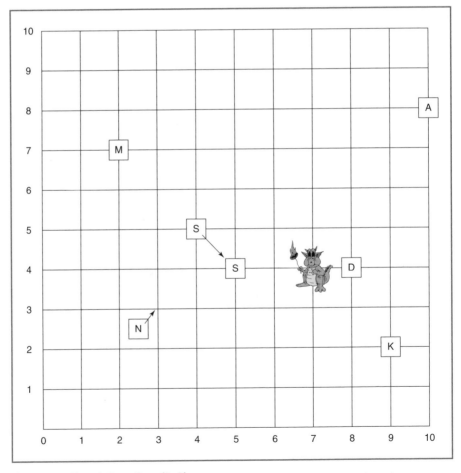

Figure 3–7 *Blazer's Game Board in Play*

next turn, Carlos plots (7,4) on the large grid. Blazer flips the power switch on the projector and the dragon icon appears right where Carlos has placed his X. The entire class cheers, and Blazer does his happy dance! The students beg for another game, but Blazer has to be on his way. Ms. Lawrence thanks Blazer, puts her notes aside, and continues with the math lesson for the day.

Identifying the Error Patterns

Figure 3–8 represents Ms. Lawrence's notes on the Blazer activity.

▶ Noah (N) named the coordinates (3,3) but placed his X in a space rather than at a point of intersection.

▶ Both Alicia (A) and Khari (K) only considered the previous clue rather than all the clues provided thus far. Alicia went northeast of Noah's point (3,3) but

Student	Guess	Clue	Notes
Maggie	(2, 7)	SE	✓
Noah	(3, 3)	NE	plotted space not point
Alicia	(10, 8)	SW	did not use S clue from Maggie
Khari	(9, 2)	NW	did not use N clue from Noah
Diseana	(8, 4)	W	✓
Selmin	(5, 4)	E	plotted (4, 5)
Carlos	(7, 4)	yeah!	✓

Figure 3–8 *Ms. Lawrence's Notes*

failed to stay south of Maggie's point (2,7). Additionally, Khari was southwest of Alicia's clue, but didn't stay north of (3,3) as given in Noah's clue.

▶ Selvin's error was one of the most common: he reversed the points, counting up on the *y*-axis first and then over on the *x*-axis. However, because the points 4 and 5 are so close on the grid, another interpretation is possible. Selvin may have had difficulty tracking the points along the lines on the grid and simply gotten off track.

▦ *What the Research Says*

The National Council of Teachers of Mathematics expects students to be able to specify location and describe spatial relationships using coordinate geometry. Students in grades 3 through 5 should specifically be able to:

■ Describe location and movement using common language and geometric vocabulary.

■ Make and use coordinate systems to specify locations and describe paths.

■ Find the distance between points along horizontal and vertical lines of a coordinate system.

"Coordinate systems are an extremely important form of representation" (Van de Walle 2007, 437). This important idea translates into students' ability to analyze other geometric ideas such as transformations. Later, coordinate geometry plays a crucial role in the representation of algebraic equations.

▦ *Ideas for Instruction*

Strategies and activities that enable students to describe location, direction, and distance accurately and efficiently range from informal discussions and vocabulary development to formal and specific mechanics of navigating a coordinate grid.

▶ Encourage students to articulate verbal descriptions of location, direction, and distance related to current or future positions. Generate a list of vocabulary words for each of the three categories, such as:

- Location: *over, under, behind, between, above, below*
- Direction: *left, right, up, down, north, south, east, west, diagonal, clockwise*
- Distance: *near, far, long, short, inches, miles*

Using these words, create (or have students create) a series of steps for reaching a specific destination—how to get from your seat to the sink or from the classroom to the playground—and let students act them out. When students generate directions for others to follow or attempt to follow the directions of their peers, they become aware of the importance of direction and distance when seeking location. It provides a logical connection to measurement as well.

▶ Ask questions that require students to consider a variety of perspectives within a grid. With a small group, construct a grid on a large piece of graph paper. Let each student choose a unique game piece and place it on the grid. Students should name the location and then respond to such questions as:

- How would you describe your location compared to mine?
- How far are you from the origin?
- Which is the shortest path for you to reach another student?
- Do you share a coordinate with anyone else?

▶ Introduce activities in which students plot points and/or spaces. In "Where's Blazer?" students plot points. However, in commercial games like Connect Four™ and Battleship™, students name spaces. It is important for students to have experiences with both and to recognize that the labels on the *x*- and *y*-axes determine whether a point or a space needs to be plotted.

▶ Make connections to real-world applications using stories and maps:

- Have students help plan an upcoming field trip. Use maps to find the destination, plan the direction needed to travel, determine the distance using the scale, and calculate the approximate time of arrival.
- Have students plan a scavenger hunt. Let them draw maps and provide clues for each stop along the path to the final treasure.
- Use a city street map (grid) to explore the fact that there are a number of ways to get from one place to another, all covering the same distance.

▶ Anticipate tracking difficulties and make tools available. Pipe cleaners work well for plotting points: one is used as a place holder for the vertical line segment, the second for the horizontal line segment. The point of intersection is the desired point. Strips (cut from translucent folders) may be used in the same manner when plotting spaces (see Figure 3–9). (Students could also use a crayon or marker to achieve the same visual effect.)

▶ Design a visual cue to help students recall that points are plotted in the sequence of over first, and then up. Mathematicians have established standards of mechanics so everyone can work within the same system. A small index card like that shown in Figure 3–10 is a helpful prop for students needing such assistance until they have more experience with the coordinate grid.

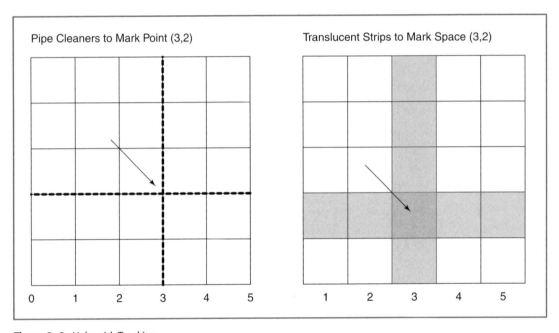

Figure 3-9 *Help with Tracking*

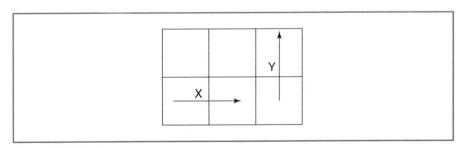

Figure 3-10 *Visual Cue Card*

▶ Expand the coordinate grid to include negative values when students are ready (perhaps just two quadrants first and then four). Working with all four quadrants of the Cartesian plane provides a larger medium for the application of symmetry, congruence, and transformations.

▪▫ Questions to Ponder
▫▪

1. How can you provide meaningful opportunities for students to navigate a coordinate grid and describe location, direction, and distance? How can they be involved in the construction of such systems?

2. Think about the errors your students make when they are naming or plotting points. What questions can you ask to diagnose the misconception?

⬛ Applying Reflection

Mr. Whittier's students have just completed a unit on congruence, symmetry, reflections, translations, and rotations, as well as an assessment designed to reveal their understanding of the material.

About one-third of the class misidentified the image in the first question (see Figure 3–11) as a horizontal reflection.

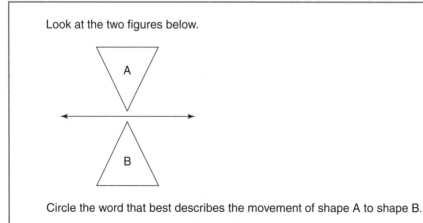

Figure 3–11 *Misidentified Reflection*

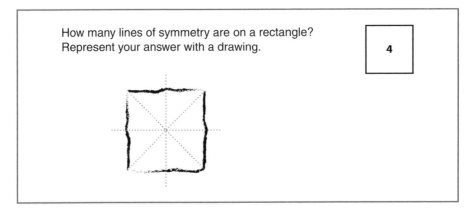

How many lines of symmetry are on a rectangle?
Represent your answer with a drawing.

4

Figure 3–12 *One Student's Response*

What does this say about their interpretation of the movement from shape A to shape B? Could the line of reflection have anything to do with their error?

The question shown in Figure 3–12 asks how many lines of symmetry there are on a rectangle. Mr. Whittier expected students to say two lines of symmetry, but many responded four lines of symmetry.

Were these students wrong? Was it a confusing question? How would you have graded these students' response?

▪▪ *Identifying the Error Pattern*

Students in Mr. Whittier's classroom mistakenly identified the horizontal line of reflection as the name of the reflection shown. These students mistakenly focused on the horizontal representation of the reflection line rather than on the movement of the figures. This is likely to happen when students complete a lot of paper/pencil tasks rather than use materials, which allow them to *feel* the movement. Many textbooks and worksheets prematurely require students to manipulate figures visually as they name and describe transformations.

What about the students who identified a rectangle as having four lines of symmetry? Mr. Whittier confessed that he at first thought they were wrong. When he looked at their work, however, he knew their response was definitely correct! They justified their answer by drawing a square, which is a special rectangle, and drew four lines of symmetry. Textbooks and worksheets often focus on narrow examples of shapes, perhaps showing only rectangles with two long sides and two short sides.

Geometry is dense with vocabulary and definitions. Many of us were taught geometric ideas in a very isolated way, which limits our understanding. How it was taught to teachers often becomes how teachers then teach it! This may perpetuate misconceptions from generation to generation.

What the Research Says

The National Council of Teachers of Mathematics recommends that all students, prekindergarten through grade 12, apply transformations and use symmetry to analyze mathematical situations (NCTM 2000, 96).

In prekindergarten through grade 2 all students should be able to:

▶ Recognize and apply slides, flips, and turns.

▶ Recognize and create shapes that have symmetry.

In grades 3–5 all students should be able to:

▶ Predict and describe the results of sliding, flipping, and turning two-dimensional shapes.

▶ Describe a motion or a series of motions that will show that two shapes are congruent.

▶ Identify and describe line and rotational symmetry in two- and three-dimensional shapes and designs.

"Younger students generally 'prove' (convince themselves) that two shapes are congruent by physically fitting one on top of the other. But students in grades 3–5 can develop greater precision as they describe the motions needed to show congruence ('turn it 90° or 'flip it vertically, then rotate it 180°')" (NCTM 2000, 167). These experiences prepare children to later be able to visualize and explain what happens when a shape is reflected or rotated.

Young children also create pictures with rotational symmetry using, for example, pattern blocks. But they will have difficulty explaining what they did and recognizing that the figure shows rotational symmetry. These informal explorations are important because they prepare students to be able to understand and describe rotational symmetry in later grades.

Providing concrete materials and introducing paper-folding activities are important; however, technological experiences enhance students' understandings of transformations, symmetry, and congruence. This will be further discussed on pages 99–100.

▪▪ *Ideas for Instruction*

To provide many and varied opportunities for your students to have a richer understanding of transformational geometry, symmetry, and congruence:

▶ Allow young students to role-play flips, slides, and turns with their bodies. These experiences help children recognize how an object has changed position but its properties have remained the same. They will also strengthen their position-in-space perception (for example, students sit on floor with legs crossed and *slide* backward on floor). "When children have experiences with movement in the space around them, they develop spatial memory, or the ability to picture the relationships of objects in the world" (Irons and Diezmann 2008, 1).

▶ Let students explore puzzles, pattern blocks, attribute blocks, or tangram puzzles. They will naturally use transformations when they create pictures or designs using these materials. Asking them to explain how their design or picture was made reinforces transformational vocabulary.

▶ Introduce problems that require students to apply transformations by flipping (reflecting), sliding (translating), and turning (rotating). For example, ask students to find all the possible arrangements for five connected squares (a pentomino). Two rules apply: at least one whole side of a square must touch a whole side of another square, and each arrangement must be different or unique. Students will need to reflect, translate, and rotate these squares as they check each arrangement to ensure that it has not already been identified. This will certainly cause them to think about congruence!

▶ Let intermediate students use concrete materials to model vertical and horizontal reflections across a line of reflection. Place pattern blocks or sets of tangram puzzles in a center area. Provide a line of reflection template (see Figure 3–13) for students to explore how these manipulatives appear when *reflected vertically* over a horizontal axis of reflection or *reflected horizontally* over a vertical axis of reflection.

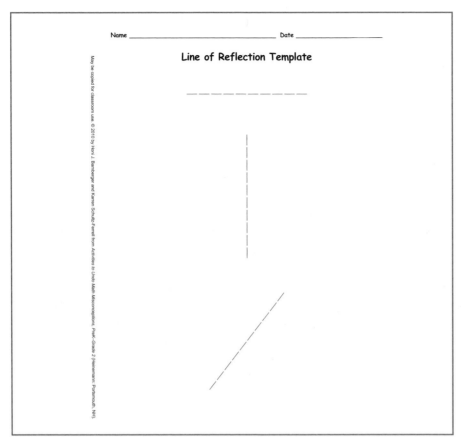

Name _____   Date _____

Line of Reflection Template

Figure 3–13 *Line of Reflection Template*

▶ Use rotation tools. Ask students to cut out a shaded figure that is congruent to an unshaded figure on a template, attach it on top of the unshaded figure using a brad, and rotate it around the brad to view its position at different points.

▶ Let students explore transformations using a variety of computer programs. These experiences require students to use spatial reasoning, help develop spatial orientation, and strengthen eye-hand coordination. The National Council of Teachers of Mathematics provides many web links to a number of these programs on their Illuminations site.

▶ Show examples and nonexamples of symmetrical designs and pictures.

▶ Model placing a mirror on a design or picture so that it is perpendicular to the table to show a symmetrical reflection. Once students are familiar with how to hold the mirror, place several mirrors in a center area along with pictures so they can explore symmetry.

▶ Have students, using pattern blocks, make a design on one side of a fold on a sheet of paper. Once the design is created, ask them to trace around the individual blocks in the design. Partners exchange papers and recreate a reflected design on the other side of the fold to demonstrate symmetry.

▶ Present a vertical line of symmetry first, when students are creating symmetrical designs or pictures. Later, provide opportunities for students to work with horizontal and diagonal lines of symmetry.

▶ Introduce paper-folding activities. Younger students might fold a sheet of paper in half, apply paint in random dabs or in a design, refold paper, and finally unfold paper to reveal a symmetrical design. Older students could also fold paper in half, cut out a design on the fold, and open up the paper to reveal a symmetrical design. Intermediate students can fold a variety of paper shapes and locate all the lines of symmetry in the shape.

▶ Have students create symmetrical designs or pictures on geoboards. Geoboards also enable students to experience rotational symmetry concretely. They make a design or picture and predict what it might look like when turned or rotated a quarter or half turn. They record their prediction on dot geoboard paper and check it by turning the geoboard.

Questions to Ponder

1. How will you change the way you are currently teaching transformations? If you feel a change is not necessary, explain what you are currently doing to help students understand this concept.

2. What is one task that has helped your students understand the idea of symmetry? Is there a way you will change the task to provide students with a richer understanding of symmetry? Describe your enhancement.

Solving Spatial Problems

The students entering Mr. Elliott's classroom notice a sweet scent. Chins rise and eyes widen as students sniff the air, attempting to identify the familiar smell.

"Marshmallows, I smell marshmallows!" Levi announces.

Other students nod in agreement. Speculation spreads as students brainstorm why today's agenda might include such a treat. After backpacks are put away, field trip money is collected, and students are settled, Mr. Elliott starts the day's math lesson.

"Let's brainstorm a list of vocabulary words we have been using during our study of geometry."

After a few minutes of quiet thinking, students talk quietly in small groups to gather additional ideas before finally sharing with the entire class. Mr. Elliott records each term on a flipchart at the front of the room as students describe activities from previous days.

"We used pattern blocks for symmetry," Jason says.

"We learned to use the compass to draw circles," adds Anna.

"The geoboards were fun for making different quadrilaterals," Desean contributes.

The list continues to grow for several more minutes, and then Mr. Elliott distributes preassembled math kits to each table. The kits contain multilink cubes, mini-marshmallows, toothpicks, and task cards with pictures of three-dimensional figures. Each white task card has a picture of a pyramid or a prism. Each green task card depicts a structure constructed from linking cubes.

Mr. Elliott tells the class to build the three-dimensional figures on the white cards using the marshmallows and toothpicks and to build the three-dimensional figures on the green cards using the multilink cubes.

The students are eager to begin. Mr. Elliott monitors student progress as they assemble their figures and talk with their classmates. He is drawn to Michael's first finished work (see Figure 3–14).

"Michael, do you know the name of this figure?"

"No, but I made it look just like the card."

"You're right, it does look exactly like the card. What if I told you that was the picture of a cube?" Mr. Elliott pulls a cube from a collection of geometric solids.

Michael glances from the rectangular prism to the task card with the sketch of the cube to his figure made of marshmallows and toothpicks. After several seconds he picks up the cube, rotates it a few times, and compares it to the

Figure 3–14 *Michael's Model of the Cube*

task card. "Oh, I see it now!" He immediately begins readjusting the marshmallows and toothpicks.

When Mr. Elliott returns several moments later, he tells Michael that the toothpicks represent the edges and the marshmallows represent the vertices on his model. Pleased with his finished product, Michael reaches for a second task card.

Molly constructs three geometric solids using the marshmallows and toothpicks, then chooses a green task card with diagrams of a front, top, and side view. She connects several blocks to mimic each diagram but is unable to figure out how to connect them to make a single figure matching the views on the task card (see Figure 3–15).

Figure 3–15 *Molly's Views of a Single Solid Figure*

William, who is sitting next to her, offers to lend a hand. Together, they flip and rotate the pieces, trying to find a way for them to connect and make sense. Becoming frustrated, they ask Mr. Elliott for some advice and guidance.

▪▪ *Identifying the Error Pattern*

Michael, Molly, and William were unable to build three-dimensional figures from the two-dimensional representations provided on the task cards. They saw the two-dimensional representation but could not visualize a unique three-dimensional figure. Michael lacked a mental image of a rectangular prism (in this case a cube). After Mr. Elliott prompted him with the actual solid, he was able to make the connection. Molly and William could not mentally manipulate the three link-cube constructions Molly had assembled to form a single figure.

▦ *What the Research Says*

The van Hieles propose instruction rather than maturation as the most significant factor contributing to the development of geometric thought (Burger and Shaughnessy 1986). This proposal is significant in that some adults believe they are "just not good at" spatial reasoning. The van Hieles contend that these skills can be enhanced through meaningful experiences. "Any activity that requires students to think about a shape mentally, to manipulate or transform a shape mentally, or to represent a shape as it is seen visually will contribute to the development of students' visualization skills" (Van de Walle 2007, 443).

We have experienced this phenomenon firsthand. Ben, a fifth grader, easily completed a worksheet depicting rectangular prisms with the three dimensions labeled, accurately finding the volume for each using the formula he was taught. However, when handed a cereal box and asked to find the volume, Ben could identify only two of the dimensions. He turned and rotated the box with confusion as he attempted to find a third value. Concepts involving three-dimensional figures cannot be taught effectively through experiences limited to two-dimensional representations. Students must be able to move flexibly between two and three dimensions. You need to plan your instruction accordingly and seek out resources appropriate for such purposes.

▦ *Ideas for Instruction*

▶ Provide opportunities for students to develop their mind's eye. Flash an image on an overhead projector for several seconds. Give students several seconds to draw what they saw. Then, show the image again so they can check their drawings against the original. It's best to use images that are familiar to students or resemble familiar objects, so they can make a connection to prior visual experiences. Begin with simple pictures and move to more complex designs (see Figure 3–16 for a few examples).

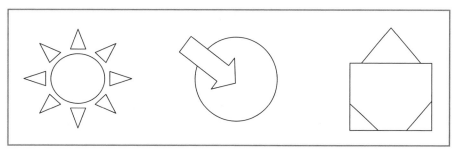

Figure 3–16 *Draw What You Saw*

▶ Allow students to manipulate materials and build structures using a variety of manipulatives: multilink cubes, wooden blocks, and connecting cubes. Ask them to describe their movements and the end products. These descriptions help learners develop a more extensive vocabulary of geometric terms.

▶ Present small groups of students with several plane diagrams (nets) and the geometric solids that result when the nets are cut and folded. Challenge the students to match each net to the solid they predict the net will form. Then have students confirm their predictions by cutting and folding the nets. Alternatively, instruct students to trace each face of a solid and form their own nets, cut them out, and fold them to form solids congruent with the original geometric figure.

▶ Project a geometric solid so that students see the shape of only a single face (conceal the solid using an upright file folder). Continue projecting the remaining faces of the solid, one at a time. Allow students to guess the name of the solid after each face is revealed. Discuss how the possibilities decrease as more faces are revealed. Ask them why it could or could not be various geometric solids. This activity helps students make a connection between the shapes of the faces and the three-dimensional solid the faces form.

▶ Let students make two-dimensional representations of three-dimensional figures using Cartesian or isometric graph paper (available free online). Cartesian graph paper is identified by its two perpendicular sets of lines forming a square grid. Isometric graph paper has three sets of parallel lines representing length, width, and height forming a grid of equilateral triangles (see Figure 3–17).

Geometry

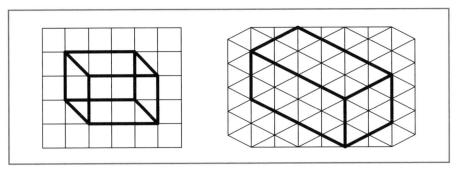

Figure 3–17 *Drawing 3-D Figures*

Provide puzzles based on:

■ Pictures/outlines of animals filled in with tans

■ Designs/patterns using pattern blocks

■ A complete set of pentominoes

■ GeoReflectors™

▶ Introduce students to real-world applications of two-dimensional drawings such as blueprints, house plans, or aerial-view photographs. Show one view of a solid and ask students to sketch the other views.

▶ Give students sets of cards showing the top, front, and side view of figures made with connecting cubes and have them construct the figures using these visual clues. Or have students make their own figures and create the corresponding clue cards showing each view.

▶ Look for geometric shapes and figures in works of art. For example:

■ *The Traveler*, by Liubov Popova

■ *Composition with Red, Blue, and Yellow*, by Piet Mondian

■ *Brooklyn Bridge*, by Joseph Stella

■ *Three Musicians*, by Pablo Picasso

■ *Cubi Series*, by David Smith

■ *Broken Obelisk*, by Barnett Newman

■ *Hand with Reflecting Sphere*, by M. C. Escher

■■ *Questions to Ponder*

1. What tools and materials are available at your school to enhance your instruction of geometry concepts? What may be needed to enhance your collection?

2. It is important for students to develop a strong vocabulary when studying geometry. How can you effectively incorporate vocabulary development into your instruction of spatial problem solving?

4 Measurement

Although measurement receives short shrift in many mathematics curriculums, it is more solidly based in the real world than any other area. "Measurement is justifiably seen as important because it provides the main route to the application of mathematics to quantities in all daily life, science, and technology practice" (Ryan and Williams 2007, 90). According to the National Council of Teachers of Mathematics, "It bridges two main areas of school mathematics—geometry and number" (NCTM 2000, 103). Indeed, it is intertwined throughout all the other mathematics content standards and integrated into other disciplines as well.

It's important that students understand an object's measurable attributes. They need to know *what* to measure before they can measure successfully. Many young children try to measure the area of a shape by using a ruler. Their error is in not knowing that a ruler measures length but not area. Weight cannot be measured with a ruler and neither can the passage of time. These understandings support other measurement ideas.

Reading an Analog Clock

Third-grade teacher, Mr. Mason, plans to begin the year by teaching his students to tell time to the minute and having them solve elapsed-time problems. In kindergarten these students learned about time in relation to the calendar: days of the week; today, yesterday, and tomorrow and the months of the year. In first grade they identified various whole-hour times on an analog clock and matched the analog hour designations with the hour indicator on a digital clock. In second grade they practiced telling time to the hour and half-hour on an analog clock and learned there are 5 minutes between each numeral. Some of his students are able to tell time down to 5-minute intervals. Mr. Mason begins his first math lesson.

"What do you know about the months of the year?"

"There are 12 months in a year," Nicolas answers.

"What are those 12 months?"

"There are 7 days, there are 7 days, there are 7 days in a week," Bryan sings. "Wait—that's days in a week, not months in a year." Other students say the name of the month in which their birthday falls.

"They know less than I thought about the months of the year," Mr. Mason thinks to himself. He tries a different tack. "What is measured when we are telling time?"

No one answers. Finally Sophia says, "We're telling the time."

"Yes, but how is time measured?" No one seems to know. Mr. Mason makes another mental note about the knowledge gaps of these eight-year-olds. "Let's talk about the clock." Using a battery-operated analog clock, he shows students different times on the hour. They answer correctly every time. When he moves the hands to half-hour times, most students can say the time but seem unaware why it's read as "four thirty" or "half past four." Next he sets the hands at 2:45. Things deteriorate:

"Nine fifteen."

"A quarter after nine."

"A quarter to two."

"A quarter to three."

"Fifteen minutes before two."

"Fifteen minutes before three."

"Nine minutes past two."

▉▉ *Identifying the Error Pattern*

There are many reasons these students may have provided the incorrect time when shown 2:45:

- They may have confused the minute hand with the hour hand ("nine fifteen" or "quarter after nine").

- They may be reading the hour numerals as minutes ("nine minutes past two").

- They may not know when to use "to the hour" versus "after the hour" or "past the hour."

- They may not realize that like a number line, until the next hour is reached, all minutes up to that point refer to the previous hour.

▉▉ *What the Research Says*

Very young children come to understand the concept of time passing, the cyclical pattern of the days of the week and the months of the year, in the context of holidays, birthdays, or special subjects studied on specific days of the week. But fully understanding how to read the hour and minute hands of an analog clock demands a "conscious switching for quarter and half turns in relation to either the hour past or the hour approaching" (Ryan and Williams 2007, 99). Later, these clockwise fractions of a turn need to be converted into fifteen-, thirty-, and forty-five-minute intervals. To complicate matters, students need to learn to read an analog clock both clockwise (forty-five minutes past a given hour) and counterclockwise (fifteen minutes before the next hour). These skills are hard to master, especially given the nondecimal nature of time.

"Measuring time causes problems for children right through the primary school" (Doig et al. 2006). Confusion over the hour and minute hands, the language associated with time (*quarter past*, *quarter of*, *half past*), and the fractions associated with periods of time create all sorts of problems. By the intermediate grades elapsed time can be more than a challenge for many students.

In *Connect to Standards 2000: Making the Standards Work at Grade 2* (Fennell et al. 2000), the authors suggest that when first introducing how to tell time on an analog clock, teachers use only the hour hand, so that students learn its relative position as time passes: when the hour is half over, the hour hand is halfway between two numerals. Also, taking the numerals from an analog clock and placing them on a horizontal number line, 1 through 12, helps teachers demonstrate what quarter past the hour, half past the hour, and quarter to the next hour look like. Students need to have a sense of the fractional parts of the hour that have passed before getting into the number of minutes these fractional parts represent.

Ryan and Williams (2007) found that only 25 percent of the eight-year-olds in their study were able to read an analog clock correctly to the quarter hour. Thirty-one percent "misread the hands of the clock" and only 11 percent were able to read "quarter to" the next hour (189). Students who erred commonly read the time as being the numeral closest to the hour hand. These same researchers found that many eight-year-olds thought there were a hundred minutes in an hour, rather than sixty.

In *Understanding Mathematics in the Lower Primary Years* (1997), Haycock and Cockburn indicate that part of the problem students have learning to tell time and grasping the passage of time is "the multitude of words relating to time": "how long, second, minute, hour, day, week, fortnight, month, quarter, year, leap year, decade, century, season, spring, summer, autumn, winter, weekend, term, lifetime, sunrise, sunset, past, present, future, evening, midnight, noon, earlier, prior, following, never, always, once, eventually, instantly, in a jiffy, meanwhile, sometime, sooner, during" (1997, 103–104).

▪▪ *Ideas for Instruction*

▶ Help prekindergarten and kindergarten students learn about things that happen in the *morning*, *afternoon*, *evening*, and *night* and realize this is a repeating pattern:

- Ask them to draw pictures of things they do in the morning, at home or at school.

- Encourage them to share things they will be doing "later" in the day.

- Be sure they learn when their birthday will be and in what month it occurs; then celebrate each birthday, reinforcing the season and what people wear during the season.

- Remember that while songs help early learners name the days of the week and the months of the year, learning the songs doesn't necessarily mean that they "know" the days of the week or the months of the year.

▶ Help students become familiar with a variety of clock faces, both analog and digital:

- Bring in different types of clocks and have them make observations about them.

- Begin with the hour hand only. Talk about things that happen at certain hours of the day, and have students observe where the hour hand is pointing.

- Play "Complete the Clock" (see *Activities to Undo Math Misconceptions, Grades PreK–2*, page 86), a game in which students count the pips on number cubes and place the resulting numeral in its correct position on a clock face.

▶ Make a human clock. Distribute the numerals 1–12 among twelve students (one each). Position the student who has the 12 and ask the class where the 6 should go. Have that student stand in the correct spot, and then do the same thing with the 3, then the 9. Then ask the students who have the numerals 1, 2, 4, 5, 7, 8, 10, and 11 to stand where they belong. Encourage a class discussion. Spread out the students who are creating the clock so another student can be the "hour hand" by lying down on the floor, clasping his hands together, and holding his arms above his head (see Figure 4–1).

Call out times and have the "hour hand" point to the appropriate numeral.

▶ Take a picture of any analog clock and glue it onto cardstock. Then cut the clock into 12 congruent parts to create a puzzle for students to piece back together. This activity will help them remember the order of the numerals on the clock—certain numerals come after other numerals. These same puzzle

Figure 4–1 *Human Clock*

pieces can be laid out horizontally in a number line. Ask what numbers come *before* and *after* other numbers.

▶ Introduce time on the half-hour using a clock that has an hour hand only. Place the hour hand between two numerals and ask students to describe where it is. They'll probably say, "It's between the 3 and the 4." Ask whether it is halfway between 3 and 4. Do this with several other contiguous numbers. Returning to the first example, ask, "Is the hour hand past the 3 or past the 4?" (If students are unfamiliar with the term *past*, tell them that *after* means the same thing.) Students will say that it is past the 3 but not yet up to the 4. Tell them that a clock that has the hour hand in this position is read as "half past 3." Give them several more examples in which they can practice using the "half past" terminology.

▶ Still using the hour-hand-only clock, show "a quarter after" and "three quarters after." Use a circle partitioned into fourths to show the meaning of these phrases and the relationship between them.

▶ Introduce telling time by five-minute intervals with the following activity. You will need:

   ■ Twelve white five-by-seven-inch index cards
   ■ Twelve yellow, pink, blue, or green three-by-five-inch index cards
   ■ Sixty sticky dots, fifteen each in four colors
   ■ Paper fasteners
   ■ A hole punch

Prepare as follows (see Figure 4–2):

   ■ Take fifteen same-color sticky dots and place five on the long side of each of three white index cards.
   ■ Do the same with the other three colors of sticky dots—place five on the long side of each of three white index cards. Punch holes in two corners of each card.
   ■ Use paper fasteners to attach all the cards so your clock is connected in a circle.
   ■ Write the numerals 1–12 on the colored index cards and place these around the clock.

Now here's the activity:

   ■ Ask twelve volunteers to come forward and stand in line, one next to the other. Have each student hold up one hand with their five fingers spread apart. Ask, "How many fingers are being held up? What could we do to fig-

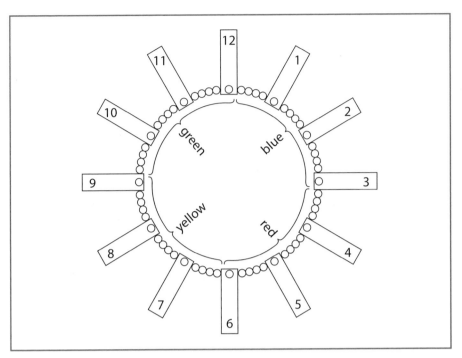

Figure 4–2 *Telling Time by Five-Minute Intervals*

ure this out?" Take their ideas, but encourage them to use counting by fives to get the answer.

- Once they have counted by fives, starting with 5, ask them which person would be 15. Ask them to share how they know this and what it means. Say, "If I am counting by fives and I stop on 45, which person in our line would I be stopping at?" Do this for several other examples.

- Then give each student in the line one of the colored numeral cards. Ask the class how these students could be arranged so that they look like a clock rather than a number line. Have students arrange themselves into a circle (be sure the 12 is opposite the 6, and the 3 and 9 are across from each other). Tell students that between each numeral on an analog clock there are five minutes. Say, "Today we are going to count around the clock in five-minute *intervals*." Show them the word *interval* and add it to the word wall, letting them know that it means "the space between things."

- Have each student with a numeral (beginning with 1) count by fives, while another student walks from 12 to 1, from 1 to 2, from 2 to 3, and so on. Ask students if they remember how many minutes have passed when the student who is walking arrives at the 6. (The answer is 30.) Tell them that the student has walked halfway around the clock. Ask, "So, how many minutes is half of an hour?"

■ Lay the index-card clock on the floor and have students place their numerals around it. Talk about the different colors of sticky dots and what this might mean. With a circle split into fourths colored in the same colors as the sticky dots, show the relationship between the fourths of the circle and the fourths of the floor clock. Ask questions about what part of an hour has passed—if fifteen minutes have passed, thirty minutes have passed, forty-five minutes have passed.

▶ Have students play a matching game in which they look at the time shown on a clock face and match it with the correct phrase as well as with the correct digital time. (See *Activities to Undo Math Misconceptions, Grades 3–5*, pages 90–91.)

▶ Play "How Many Minutes After." Students toss two numeral cubes, name the sum, draw the minute hand on a clock face to indicate that number of minutes, and write the number of minutes after the hour this refers to. (For example: If a 3 and a 4 are tossed the sum is 7. The minute hand would point to the 7 and the number of minutes after the hour would be written as 35.)

▶ Give students realistic story problems about the passage of time and what time things happen and end. Let them manipulate or draw hands on an analog clock and represent the times as they would be displayed on a digital clock. Have students explain how they arrived at their answer.

▶ Create a set of "clock dominoes" that have digital and analog times to be matched.

▶ Read a math-related children's book as a springboard into a lesson on time. Suggestions include *Pigs on a Blanket*, by Amy Axelrod (1996); *The Grouchy Ladybug*, by Eric Carle (1977); *Clocks and More Clocks*, by Pat Hutchins (1970); and *Just a Minute*, by Teddy Slater (1996).

▶ Once your "official" unit on time is over, do something every day that requires students to look at the clock and note the time.

▶ Stamp a clock face on the top of their papers and have students draw in the hands to show their starting and their finishing times. Have them write down the amount of time it took for them to complete the assignment.

1. What are some other activities that you've done in your classroom that help students learn how to tell time (on the hour, half-hour, quarter-hour, five-minute intervals, or to the minute)?

2. How can you use the technology that is already in your classroom to help students learn to tell time?

 # Determining the Value of Coins

It's September, and first-grade teacher Mrs. Baugess is preassessing her students' ability to determine the value of a set of coins. The students have worked with pennies, nickels, and dimes in kindergarten, and she wants to find out what they remember and whether any of them know what a quarter is. She gives each student a bag of coins containing a different number of dimes, nickels, pennies, or quarters, and asks them to figure out how much money is in the bags.

Nathan has 2 dimes, a nickel, and 5 pennies. He empties the coins onto his work mat and sorts them by type. He correctly counts the pennies first and states the coins have a value of 5 cents. Next he touches and counts each dime, saying, "Six, 7," and finally picks up the nickel and announces, "Eight cents." The look on his face as he says, "I thought I had more!" is priceless. He shrugs and puts the coins back into the bag.

Emily's bag contains a dime and 3 nickels. She arranges her coins in a row, beginning with the 3 nickels and placing the dime at the end. She announces she has 35 cents. Asked to explain how she figured this out, she says, "A dime is 10 cents, and a nickel is 5 cents. Ten cents is the most, so I counted these [the nickels] first, because they're the biggest. That's 30 cents. I know my tens! This [the dime] is 5 cents, because it's smaller. So I counted on 31, 32, 33, 34, 35." She is confident her answer is correct.

Morgan's bag contains 3 dimes, 1 nickel, and 6 pennies. She sorts her coins into groups on the work mat. She counts the dimes first, "Ten and 10 and 10. That's 30." She then counts 5 fingers and says, "Now I have 35, because a nickel is 5 cents. Pennies are easy." She touches her head and says, "Thirty-five," then touches each penny and says, "Thirty-six, 37, 38, 39, 40, 41. I have 41 cents in my bag."

William's bag contains a quarter and 4 pennies. He empties them onto his work mat, picks up the quarter, and correctly states its value as 25 cents. Then he puts the quarter back on the work mat and counts the pennies: "Twenty-five cents, 26 cents, 27 cents, 28 cents."

▪▪ *Identifying the Error Pattern*

John Van de Walle and LouAnn Lovin (2006) state that recognizing coins and knowing their value are not mathematical skills but rather social conventions. Children memorize the names of coins and their values through repetition. Whatever the nomenclature, it is critical that young students in the primary grades:

- Recognize coins

- Know each coin's value

- Use those values to:
  - Count sets of coins (and compare their values)
  - Determine equivalent sets of coins
  - Select coins to produce a given amount of money
  - Make change

Difficulties often begin when students begin to work with coin values.

Nathan correctly states that 5 pennies have a value of 5 cents; however, he does not identify the pennies as pennies. He counts the dimes and nickel as if they are the same objects as the pennies. He recognizes that the coins are different, because he sorts them by type, but he does not recognize that different coins have different values. His understanding of counting is still tied to one-to-one correspondence. He sees a dime as a single entity and does not yet understand that it represents 10 pennies.

Emily has memorized the values of the coins; however, she believes that a coin's size is related to its value. The bigger the coin, the more value it has. This may be because of other measurement experiences she has had. For example, when comparing two sticks composed of linked cubes, the longer stick has more cubes in it,

---

or a higher number of cubes. The difficulty here is that in our money system, the value of a coin is not proportional to its size.

Morgan has a good understanding of how to count her coins. She quickly sorts them into like groups and counts each group of coins.

William's error is a simple counting-on error. He knows a quarter has a value of 25 cents; however, he counts the first penny as 25 cents (still thinking about the value of the quarter) and continues counting the last three pennies as 26, 27, 28.

■■ *What the Research Says*

Randall Drum and Wesley Petty (1999) find that although coins are a concrete model, because their value is nonproportional to their size, they become abstract when those values are taught. They recommend that instruction include experiences in which children develop a conceptual understanding rather than memorize the names of coins and their values. (Strategies are included below.)

In their research, Douglas Clements and Julie Sarama (2004) found that it takes a long time to master money skills because children have to both count on and skip-count in different increments (fives, tens, twenty-fives)—for example, 10, 20, 25, 30, 35, 36, 37, 38. In traditional instruction, young students are often expected to use mental computation before they completely understand the concept of addition.

Van de Walle and Lovin's research (2006) reveals that in order for coin values—5, 10, 25—to make sense, students need to understand what they mean. Children look at a dime without thinking about the countable pennies it represents; in traditional instruction we point to a dime—one object—and say, "This is 10"! "A child whose number concepts remain tied to counts of objects is not going to be able to understand the values of coins" (150). Cute but inappropriate tactics to help students remember coin values only confuse children later on as they count mixed quantities of coins and compute with money amounts.

■■ *Ideas for Instruction*

The following activities help students make sense of the values of coins and how to use these values to count and compare sets of coins. They also help students identify equivalent collections of coins, select coins of a given value, and make change. Decide which activities will work best for your students based on their current understanding.

▶ Provide opportunities for students to examine real coins with a magnifying glass and describe their attributes (work with only one type of coin at a time). Create a web for each coin on which students can record these attributes. As part of the descriptions, include how many cents are in a nickel, in a dime, and in a quarter.

▶ Use children's literature to pose problems that support students' understanding of 5, 10, and 25 (lists of books are included in both activity books).

▶ Skip-count by fives, tens, and twenty-fives. Use coins to help facilitate skip counting.

▶ To help students understand 5, 10, and 25, tape a penny onto a connecting cube, a nickel onto 5 connected cubes, a dime onto 2 lengths of 5 connected cubes placed side by side, and a quarter onto 5 lengths of 5 connected cubes placed side by side.

▶ Give primary students sets of coins to count that are only a nickel and some pennies or a dime and some pennies. Later, include a set consisting of a quarter and some pennies. When students are ready, add more types of coins and more than one of each type.

▶ Play "10 Dimes" (see Figure 4–3). Two players, in turn, shake and spill two dot cubes, add up and announce the total number of dots, and place that many pennies on the penny side of their mat. (Each player has a mat.) When 10 pennies are accumulated, they are exchanged for a dime, which is placed on the dime side of the mat. Following each player's turn, he or she states the total value of the coins on his or her mat. Game continues until one of the players has 10 dimes.

▶ When students are counting money, give a signal to indicate a shift in the amount by which to skip-count (for example, from tens to fives). Use only two types of coins initially. For example, using a set of three dimes and two nickels, point to the dimes first and ask students to count (10 cents, 20 cents, 30 cents). Hold up your hand (to indicate a pause) and bring it back down. Then point to nickels and continue to count (35 cents, 40 cents). Gradually add additional types of coins. Each time pause between counts that require a different type of counting. (See *Teaching Student-Centered Mathematics, Grades K–3*, Van de Walle and Lovin 2006, 151, for more detail.)

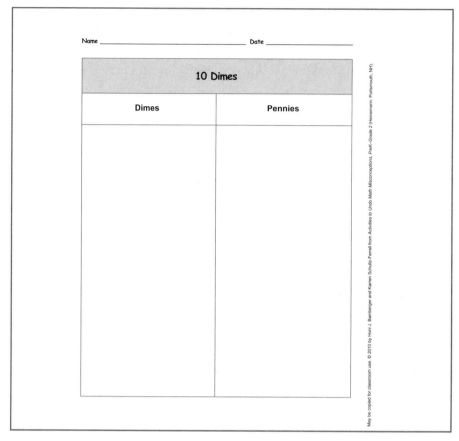

Name _____   Date _____

10 Dimes	
Dimes	**Pennies**

Figure 4–3 *10 Dimes Game Board*

▶ Ask students to place coins in order, from those with the highest value to those with the lowest. First, check students' abilities to put numerals in order beginning with the greatest number (for example, if you give students the numbers 1, 10, 1, 5, 25, 10, 1, and 5, they would line them up as 25, 10, 10, 5, 5, 1, 1, 1). This exercise helps them organize coin sets before determining their value.

▶ Play "Exchanging for a Quarter." Give partners a bag of real coins containing pennies, nickels, dimes, and quarters. Partners shake and spill a dot cube and take that number of pennies. When they have enough pennies, they exchange them for a nickel; then they exchange 2 nickels for a dime and 2 dimes and a nickel for a quarter. (They can exchange coins only when it is their turn.) Game continues until one of the partners is able to trade for a quarter. This reinforces the different combinations of coins that make up 25 cents.

▶ Using hundreds charts, show students the number of pennies in a nickel, a dime, and a quarter (Drum and Petty 1999, 264–68; also see *Activities to Undo Math Misconceptions, Grades PreK–2*).

▶ Encourage students to mentally add numbers that represent the values of different coins. For example, randomly write the numbers 10, 10, 5, 5, and 5 on the board and ask students to add them mentally. Vary the order of the numbers each time, and always use 1, 5, 10, or 25.

Questions to Ponder

1. What difficulties do your students encounter when they are counting coins? How will you help them overcome these errors or misunderstandings?

2. What new strategy can you implement to help students count coins or make change?

 # Units Versus Numbers

It's February, and Mr. Miller's second-grade class is about halfway through a measurement unit. They are getting ready to use standard 12-inch rulers to measure pictures of objects on a worksheet.

The students appear to be lining up their rulers correctly, and they proceed quickly down the page, but many measurements are incorrect. Asked about her measuring technique, Liz explains with confidence, "You have to match the end of the ruler with the end of the picture to get it right." Other students use similar logic to explain what they are doing.

As he measures the picture of a pencil, Henry counts every mark on his ruler, beginning with the first, which is actually 0, although it isn't labeled. He states that the pencil is 41 inches long (it's really 3 and a half inches). He seems puzzled. Asked how he got his measurement, he replies, "You line up the ruler and start counting. I started counting here [0] and counted these lines until I got the end of the pencil. But I thought the pencil was shorter."

Madison is measuring the picture of a notepad, which is 5 inches long. She announces the notepad is 6 inches and is pleased with her answer. Asked to show how she got it, she places her ruler along the picture of the notepad and explains, "The 1 mark is at the beginning of the notepad. Just count until you get to the end of the picture; 6 is at the end."

Many students are "touching and counting" the whole number markings on their ruler. However, the picture of the pencil is 3 and a half inches long, and some students approximate it visually. Nate explains, "I counted each number on the ruler: 1, 2, 3. But the pencil is longer than 3. It looks like it's halfway between the 3 and the 4. I think that's 3 and a half." He gets the correct measurement yet relies on the whole-number markings.

Mr. Miller is both disappointed and surprised that some of his students cannot use a ruler appropriately to obtain accurate measurements. Why do you think the students are having difficulty? What misunderstandings are they demonstrating? Have your students experienced some of these same difficulties?

Identifying the Error Pattern

"When measuring with a ruler of this type, children must deal directly with the fact that the length of an object is the number of units (spaces, not marks, on the ruler) between the beginning point and the end point" (Hiebert 1984, 24). The explanations offered by the students in this class sound like restated "procedures" they have heard others say and may have misinterpreted. They line up the ruler in a procedural way, the end of the ruler next to the end of the picture, paying little attention to markings on the ruler. But the base point on the rulers these students are using begins a short distance from the edge of the ruler. (Perhaps the markings on the rulers students used in first grade did begin at the edge of the ruler.) Lining up the ruler in this manner always produces an incorrect measurement.

Henry counts every mark on his ruler, ignoring whole numbers at the inch markings, and obtains an unreasonable result. Although he isn't confident about his answer, he isn't sure why he gets what he does. He views measuring as a procedural counting task and doesn't see the whole number markings as meaningful. He simply counts all the marks! He doesn't understand that the length being measured is defined by units, or spaces.

Madison begins at 1 and therefore measures the notepad incorrectly as 6 inches. This is a common error. Children have been counting since they were toddlers, and in the majority of these experiences, counting begins at 1. Madison ignores the unlabeled markings and the unit before the 1. She focuses on the labeled numbers rather than the units, or spaces, between numbers to obtain her measurement.

Nate measures the pencil correctly, but does he understand the meaning of the task? He lines up the ruler correctly (noting that the 0 begins a short distance from the edge) and then begins to count procedurally as he touches each whole number on the ruler. When he gets to the "messy" measuring at the end of the pencil, he does pay attention to the unit, or space, between 3 and 4. He visually estimates the left-over part of the pencil's length, but he is still relying on whole numbers.

▨ *What the Research Says*

Linear measurement includes thinking about how long, how tall, how wide, how thick, or how far around something is. Intuitive ideas about measurement are developed in early childhood as students use their perception to compare the length, width, and height of objects. Errors appear when children believe that "longer is more" or begin working with specific measurement tools, such as a ruler.

Constance Kamii (2006) says that teachers almost always ask students to produce a number about a single object rather than asking them to compare two or more objects (156). This is true of traditional textbooks as well. The purpose for measurement is not immediately obvious when children measure numerous isolated pictures of objects. It's not surprising they view these as procedural tasks only.

In *Engaging Young Children in Mathematics* (2004), Clements and Sarama describe foundational concepts related to length measurement (301–302):

▶ *Partitioning.* Dividing an object into same-size units. That this is not obvious to children becomes apparent when they are asked what the hash marks on a ruler mean. A child who does not understand partitioning of length sees the 3 on a standard ruler as a hash mark rather than as the end of a space that is divided into 3 equal-size units.

▶ *Unit iteration.* Iterating a unit repeatedly along the length of an object. Children with little understanding of this concept often leave gaps between subsequent units or even overlap the units.

▶ *Transitivity.* The understanding that if the length of one object is equal to the length of a second object, which is equal to the length of a third object that cannot be directly compared with the first, the first and third objects are also the same length.

▶ *Conservation.* The understanding that as an object moves, its length does not change.

▶ *Accumulation of distance.* When you iterate a unit along an object's length and count the iterations, the number words convey the space covered by all units counted up to that point.

▶ *Relation between number and measurement.* Many children fall back on their earlier counting experiences to interpret measuring tasks (for example, beginning with 1 rather than 0). Students who simply read a ruler procedurally have not related the meaning of the number to its measurement.

"Although researchers debate the order of the development of these concepts and the ages at which they are developed, they agree that these ideas form the foundation for measurement and should be considered during any measurement instruction" (Clements and Sarama 2004, 304).

Ideas for Instruction

■ Provide many opportunities for primary students to describe the attributes of a variety of objects and what could be measured on each to determine aspects of their size.

■ Allow students to compare objects and expect them to describe the results. This reinforces vocabulary specific to measurement, such as *longer, shorter, wider, narrower*.

■ Ask students to sort a variety of objects into length groupings based on a designated marker. For example, students sort objects into three groups: objects shorter than the marker, longer than the marker, and about the same size as the marker. Once groups are sorted, ask students to order objects in each group from shortest to longest.

■ Ask students to estimate the size of an object first before measuring it. Expect students to explain why they think their estimate is reasonable. This task helps primary and intermediate students develop number sense.

■ Allow students to measure real objects rather than pictures on paper. Environmental objects force children to approximate, a more realistic application of measurement.

- Encourage students to measure the same object with a variety of nonstandard units of different sizes. This activity reinforces the importance of a unit's size and makes clear that some measurement units are more efficient. Students will develop the critical understanding that when measurement units are small, more are needed.

- Bridge nonstandard units to standard units by providing manipulatives that are a "standard" size (such as one-inch color tiles, one-centimeter cubes, Cuisenaire® Rods, base-ten blocks). For example, if you ask students to measure the length of a pencil by lining up color tiles, they will need to approximate the object's length.

- Have students make their own measuring tools (see Figure 4–4). For example, making a ruler helps students understand a ruler's purpose and realize that it's not just a preexisting tool with which to complete a procedural task. Directions for making a ruler that uses no numbers or markings (which focuses students' attention on the spaces, or units) are included in *Activities to Undo Math Misconceptions, Grades PreK–2*, page 97. Eventually have students compare the ruler they've made to a standard ruler. Ask them to describe how they are alike and how they are different. What do the numbers mean on the standard ruler? Where is the starting point on each ruler?

- Initially provide primary students with rulers that have only inch markings. Doing so supports understanding that each space (instead of a mark) on a ruler represents a unit (see Figure 4–5). Next, provide half-inch rulers and eventually one-quarter-inch rulers. This gradual exposure will better prepare students to use traditional rulers, which are filled with markings and can be quite confusing.

- Use rulers with the zero mark a short distance from the edge. This tool will force students to think about both endpoints when measuring and to focus on units (not markings) when they measure.

- Ask students to develop and explain strategies for measuring curved and crooked lines or other hard-to-measure objects, such as a door.

Figure 4–4 *Student-Made Ruler*

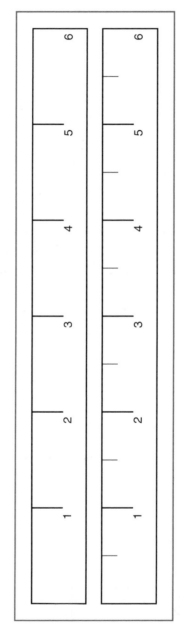

Figure 4–5 *Inch and Half-Inch Rulers*

1. What difficulties have your students had in measuring length? How will you change your instruction to avoid future misconceptions?

2. What activities or strategies can you use to help your students develop the foundational concepts described above?

Distinguishing Between Area and Perimeter

Ms. Davis is a first-year teacher who believes students need hands-on experiences when learning mathematics. She has asked her teaching coach for suggestions on how to improve the questions she asks when she is assessing student understanding. Her coach agrees to model the questioning process.

The coach arrives in the classroom during "explore time," a phrase Ms. Davis uses for the time students spend manipulating materials used in a lesson. Today they are exploring with tangrams. First they review the contents of a tangram set and describe the shape and size of each tan. Then, after reading *Grandfather Tang's Story*, by Robert Andrew Parker, they manipulate the tans to create the hawk, turtle, crocodile, and a slew of other animals from the story.

Now it's time for the students to create their own animals. There are just two conditions:

■ They must use all seven tans with no overlapping pieces.

■ All pieces must touch by more than a single point.

Ms. Davis explains that their creations will be used to explore area and perimeter, two concepts they have been working on for several days.

Centimeter grid paper, blank on the back, is on each table. Students can use the square-unit side to find the area, then flip to the blank side to measure and find the perimeter in centimeters. Students are excitedly arranging tans, tracing them, and cutting out an array of creatures. Ms. Davis observes as the coach circulates, asking questions.

"How do you think the area of your animal will compare with Jason's?" the coach asks Rasheed.

"I think Jason's will be more, because his snake is longer than my dog."

"How many tans did you use?

"Seven."

"The same 7 pieces as Jason?"

"Yes."

The coach asks Simone, "What strategy are you using to find the perimeter?"

"I am counting all the squares."

"How did you know to do that??"

"Because perimeter is all the squares in the middle and around the edge."

The coach moves on to Jeremy. "What would be an estimate for your perimeter?"

"Well, I think it will be the same as Barbara's."

"What makes you think so?"

"Because we had the same area, so we will have the same perimeter."

"Are your animals the same shape?"

"No, she made a cat and I made a lion, but we used the same pieces so it will be the same."

Next the coach asks Miranda what strategy she is using to find the area.

Miranda says, "I know that area equals length times width, so I can find the area of each piece and add them together."

"How are you finding the length and width of each shape?"

Miranda explains that for each triangle she measured the hypotenuse [she doesn't use this word, however] as the length and then measured from the vertex [again, she doesn't use the word but points to where the lines of the right angle intersect] to the hypotenuse as the width. For the parallelogram she measured the length of two adjacent sides and multiplied.

MATH MISCONCEPTIONS

:: Identifying the Error Patterns

Rasheed assumes that if the animals are different, the areas will also be different. He isn't aware of the conservation of area. Even after confirming that he and Jason have used the same number of congruent tans, Rasheed still maintains that the long snake has a greater area than his dog.

Simone counts all the squares to find the perimeter. She even combines portions of squares to arrive at a more precise measure. However, she has confused the definitions of area (square units within a space delineated by two dimensions) and perimeter (linear measure of one dimension).

Jeremy recognizes that he and Barbara have the same area for their animals, even though he made a lion and she made a cat. Although the overall shapes are different, it makes sense to him that the area will be the same because they have used the same pieces. He knows that arrangement does not affect area. However, Jeremy also assumes that if the area of their figures is the same, the perimeters will be the same.

Miranda attempts a more abstract method of finding area. She deals with each piece individually, applying the formula of length times width. Miranda recognized this relationship during a previous lesson when the class was constructing rectangles with tiles. She decides to apply the same formula to shapes other than rectangles, arbitrarily naming the length and width of each shape.

:: What the Research Says

The concepts of area and perimeter are first developed through comparison and the use of nonstandard units similar to linear measurement. Big ideas are that area is a measure of covering and that perimeter (length around) is a measure of distance. Area and perimeter are often taught together or in immediate succession. This combination or sequence may cause confusion, because both area and perimeter require students to consider the boundaries of the shape. "It is common fallacy to suppose that the area of a region is related to its perimeter" (Leibeck 1984).

Haycock (2001) notes that this relationship proves a contradiction to ideas of conservation. He stresses that rearranging a constant perimeter to form a new shape conserves the perimeter, but not the area. It is therefore important to provide meaningful problems that allow students to experience this phenomenon. "Through problem-solving tasks, students develop an understanding of math content and ultimately use that content understanding to find solutions to problems. Problem solving is both the process by which students explore mathematics and the goal of learning mathematics" (O'Connell 2007). It is important for students to find their own strategies and algorithms to measure specific attributes rather than simply plug numbers into formulas presented to them without context or meaning.

▪▪ *Ideas for Instruction*

▶ Allow students to explore area by covering the surface of a variety of objects with nonstandard units (for example, covering the top of a table with foam cutouts or covering the outline of a student's hand with a collection of rocks). This activity helps them see area as the amount of surface within specific boundaries. Then move on to covering surfaces using congruent units, such as index cards or multilink cubes. Using a consistent unit allows students to compare the areas of different shapes.

▶ Connect the concepts of area and perimeter to meaningful scenarios like those in children's books. *Spaghetti and Meatballs for All!*, by Marilyn Burns, is a great story for promoting discussion. It explores how the arrangement of the same number of tables (area) impacts the amount of available seating (perimeter). Make connections to science by planning a school garden. Allow students to determine how to get the greatest area given the allotted space.

▶ Give students a set amount of squares and triangles (pattern blocks work well) to use to make a tessellation. Compare the varying designs created. Compare the area of each. Discuss the notion of conservation of area. Get students to recognize that although the tessellations vary in appearance, the area is consistent for all.

▶ Use a multiplication chart to illustrate the connection between the area of a rectangle and multiplicative arrays. Figure 4–6 shows that a 4-unit times 4-unit square covers an area of 16 units. Such connections help students construct their own formulas based on their conceptual understanding rather than mimicking a formula that is simply handed to them without a context.

▶ Have students use pattern blocks or square tiles to create a variety of designs with a constant perimeter. Instruct students to compare the areas of the shapes made with like materials. Discuss what trends they notice about the area of shapes that all have the same perimeter.

▶ Have students shade, fold, or even cut square-grid paper to explore the relationship between area and the dimensions of length and width:

X	1	2	3	4	5	6	7	8	9
1	1	2	3	4	5	6	7	8	9
2	2	4	6	8	10	12	14	16	18
3	3	6	9	12	15	18	21	24	27
4	4	8	12	16	20	24	28	32	36
5	5	10	15	20	25	30	35	40	45
6	6	12	18	24	30	36	42	48	54
7	7	14	21	28	35	42	49	56	63
8	8	16	24	32	40	48	56	64	72
9	9	18	27	36	45	54	63	72	81

Figure 4–6 *Multiplication Chart Modeling Area*

- What happens to the area of a rectangle if the length is doubled?
- How is the area affected if both the length and width are doubled? Why?
- If the length and width were cut in half, what would happen to the area?

Explorations like this reveal that doubling one dimension doubles the area, but doubling both dimensions increases the area by four times the original quantity.

▶ Provide cutouts of rectangles, triangles, trapezoids, and circles and have students develop strategies for finding the area of each. Strategies may include:

- Tracing on grid paper and counting units
- Placing square tiles on the shape and counting approximate units
- Recognizing that the area of the triangle is half the area of a rectangle drawn around the triangle (see Figure 4–7)

Measurement

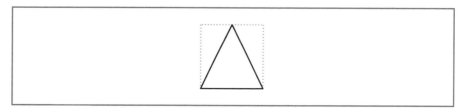

Figure 4-7 *Area of a Triangle*

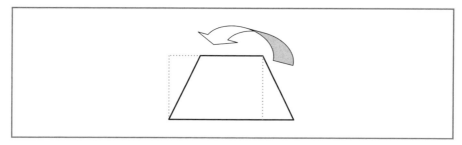

Figure 4-8 *Area of a Trapezoid*

■ Seeing that the trapezoid can be cut and manipulated to form a rectangle (see Figure 4-8).

Questions to Ponder

1. How can you help students distinguish between area and perimeter in a meaningful context?

2. What materials are available in your school to make the concepts of measurement a hands-on experience?

 Overgeneralizing Base-Ten Renaming

"That's not what you do! You need to think about the yard as feet and then the feet as inches." At a table, four fifth graders are struggling to figure out the answer to the following measurement problem (see *Activities to Undo Math Misconceptions, Grades 3–5,* page 109):

Tanisha is making headbands to sell for a fund-raiser given by her youth group. Each headband needs 7 inches of fabric. She buys 1 yard of fabric from the store, and makes a headband right away. How much fabric does she have left?

See Figure 4–9 for the answer these four students come up with.

"We knew that we had to change the yard into feet. So we wrote how many feet were in a yard. There are 3 feet in a yard. Then we changed the 3 feet into 2 feet and 10 inches by crossing off the 3 and making it a 2 and then borrowing a 10. Then we had enough inches to subtract. Ten take away 7 equals 3. So Tanisha has 2 feet and 3 inches left."

A lot of other students in the class reach this same answer; many others decide the answer is 2 feet and 5 inches. At one table everyone agrees that the answer is 9 feet and 3 inches!

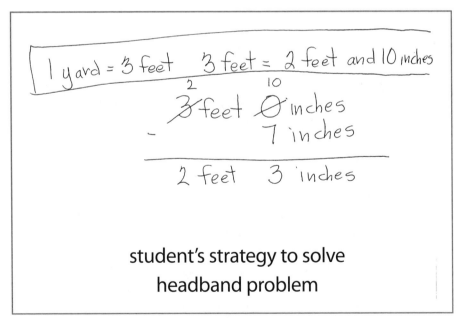

Figure 4–9 *Tanisha's Work*

▪▪ *Identifying the Error Pattern*

Misunderstandings often arise when students add and subtract measurement units. They overgeneralize what they know about place value and renaming when solving problems that involve renaming measurement units (for example, applying what they know about tens when renaming feet to inches or hours to minutes).

The students who have gotten 9 feet and 3 inches did a double incorrect renaming. They "crossed off" the 1 yard and made it 10 feet and then took 1 foot from the 10 feet, leaving 9 feet. The 1 foot they "borrowed" became a 10 (as in inches), and they then subtracted the 7 inches. What remained was 9 feet and 3 inches, an answer that doesn't remotely make sense but that an entire table of students thinks was right. They have incorrectly applied a procedure learned in an earlier grade.

Students often do this sort of thing. They watch as a teacher demonstrates how to rename (when subtracting, for example) and then practice this modeled procedure. Do they ever understand why the procedure works? Maybe some students do. But many others blindly follow what they have seen the teacher do and practice until they have the procedure down pat.

▪▪ *What the Research Says*

In *Knowing and Teaching Elementary Mathematics* (1999), Liping Ma discusses in depth the way teachers in the United States teach subtraction. She asks,

> Is a deep understanding of mathematics necessary in order to teach it? Does such a simple topic even involve a deep understanding of mathematics? Would a teacher's subject matter knowledge make any difference in his or her teaching and eventually contribute to students' learning? There is only one answer for all these questions: Yes. (2)

So what is it that teachers need to know and understand in order to teach subtraction (specifically of measurement units) with renaming so that students do not overgeneralize and assume that whenever something is renamed, a 10 is created? Students in the intermediate grades have already been introduced to subtraction with renaming. Their teachers will need to "repair" this thinking rather than be able to teach the content the best way the first time.

Teachers of third through fifth graders expect their students to enter their classrooms with some understanding of different units of measure. In a 1984 *Arithmetic Teacher* article, Jim Hiebert writes, "Effective instruction should take advantage of what children already know or are able to learn and then relate this knowledge to new concepts that might be more difficult to learn" (22–23). The best way to help students see the relationship between units of measure is by having them use measuring devices during mathematics class.

Ideas for Instruction

▶ Provide students with opportunities to explore different manipulative materials when measuring. Before solving a problem that requires a thorough understanding of renaming customary units for linear measure, these fifth graders should have explored yardsticks and rulers with inch markings. The thirty minutes of class time used to do so would have been time well spent. Some sort of observation sheet should be created so students are purposefully exploring these devices rather than just looking at them (see Figure 4–10). Questions like these give students a clearer understanding of the many ways in which units of measure can be correctly written.

After students have gone over the answers on the recording sheet as well as discussed other ways that yards and feet could be renamed, the Tanisha problem just might make more sense.

Look at the measuring tools you've been given. Then think about how you'd use this information to solve different measurement problems.

One yard is the same as _____ inches.

One foot is the same as _____ inches.

How many feet are there in 1 yard? _____ How did you figure this out?

If you had 2 feet, how many additional inches would you need to equal to 1 yard? _____ So 2 feet and _____ inches is the same as 1 yard.

If you had 1 foot, how many additional inches would you need to equal 1 yard? _____. So 1 foot and _____ inches is the same as 1 yard.

How many inches are there in 1 yard and 1 foot? _____ How did you figure this out?

How many inches are there in 1 yard and 2 feet? _____ How did you figure this out?

Five feet is the same as how many yards and how many extra feet? _____ How did you figure this out?

Figure 4–10 *Equivalent Units of Measure*

▶ Allow students time to brainstorm and then discuss strategies for solving story problems before they begin to work on answers. The Tanisha problem can be used in ways other than merely giving it to students to solve. Why not pass out the problem and have students discuss strategies for solving it? If students still have their yardsticks they've explored, some may count back 7 from 36 inches, arriving at 29 inches without having done any conscious renaming.

▶ Use these same kinds of activities whenever an addition or subtraction problem involves units of measure. Before determining how much time has elapsed between one time and another, students need to explore "geared clocks" and complete an observation sheet that looks at the different ways hours can be renamed. Just to know that 1 hour is the same as 60 minutes, or 3,600 seconds, is not enough. Could your students figure out that 1 hour is the same as 50 minutes and 600 seconds? Might they look for patterns if you gave them a sheet that had these increments written out: 60 minutes and 0 seconds equals 1 hour; 50 minutes and 600 seconds equals 1 hour; 40 minutes and 1,200 seconds equals 1 hour; and so on.

▶ Have students look for and then discuss patterns as they rename different units of measure. When customary capacity ideas for liquid measure are being reinforced, students need to figure out different ways to rename gallons. Gallons are not simply 4 quarts, or 8 pints, or 16 cups. There are many ways to rename gallons, and students need time to figure these out before solving problems that require this renaming skill.

▪▪ *Questions to Ponder*

1. What other instructional experiences will help students better understand the base-ten relationship and when (and when not) to use it for renaming?

2. What other measurement tools or materials ought to be introduced to students in third through fifth grades so they can use them to solve problems?

Data Analysis and Probability

5

K nowing about statistics and probability enables us to make practical, informed decisions based on data that have been collected and disseminated. Today more and more teachers are being asked to use the data collected from state and national assessments to inform curricular decisions.

Young children, too, need experiences collecting, organizing, displaying, and analyzing data so that statistics doesn't become a formidable concept. Interestingly, elementary teachers spend little time on this important content area, focusing the majority of their academic year on number ideas and computation. But when the number information comes from surveys developed by students and the data are compared and used to make informed decisions about topics valued by these students, the computations are embedded in a context that makes sense.

Sorting and Classifying

It's late winter, and the prekindergarten students in Mrs. Hoover's classroom are exploring a variety of materials. Children are happily counting sets of objects, building structures, and making patterns or designs. They are all using some form of sorting to help them with their task.

Mrs. Hoover is observing them informally. She first sits with Joseph at the sorting table, watching him take 10 or so attribute blocks from the box. To find out what he knows about sorting, she points to the blocks and asks him which ones go together. He thinks a moment and then with great confidence picks out 2 squares and 2 hexagons. So far so good! Then he places each hexagon on top of a square and looks up with a pleased expression. When Mrs. Hoover asks how they go together, Joseph quickly responds, "They're flowers."

Allison is also exploring the attribute blocks (see Figure 5–1). She sorts the blocks by color, assembling a group of red, then a group of yellow, and finally a group of blue.

Wondering whether Allison can sort the blocks in a different way, Mrs. Hoover places all of them back together and asks Allison to sort the blocks by shape. Allison takes a large red circle and places it in front of her, then seems confused. Mrs. Hoover asks whether there is another block that matches the large red circle. Allison places a large blue circle next to the large red circle, saying, "It's a circle like this one." Next, she places a large yellow circle and two small yellow circles in the group. Then she places a small yellow triangle with the circles and says she's done.

Figure 5–1 *Allison Explores with Attribute Blocks*

Carla and Paul are exploring a collection of lids. They each have 10 lids, and each sorts the lids he or she has into 2 groups. Mrs. Hoover asks how they have sorted their lids. Paul replies that he sorted his lids into big and little. Carla explains she sorted by bumpy and smooth. Paul looks at Carla's lids in disbelief: "They're just big and little, see?" Sorting them into groups by texture seems wrong to him.

Mrs. Hoover is puzzled. She has provided many opportunities for her students to sort throughout the school year and thought everyone was progressing well with this important mathematics concept.

Identifying the Misconceptions

When Joseph placed a hexagon over a square, Mrs. Hoover initially thought he didn't understand how to sort. But when she asked Joseph to explain how the blocks went together, he said they made a flower. He interpreted the question *Which blocks go together?* as a request to make a picture. The wording of the question confused him. Much of the language associated with sorting and classifying (*all*, *some*, *not*, *go together*, *similar*, and so on) is abstract to children in the early grades. By soliciting more information from Joseph, Mrs. Hoover realized she needed to help him learn the necessary vocabulary.

Allison began by placing the various attribute blocks into groups of red, blue, and yellow. When Mrs. Hoover asked whether she could re-sort them by shape, she appeared to be making a group of circles (a large red circle, a large blue circle, a large yellow circle, two small yellow circles), but she finished by placing a small yellow triangle in the group. When Mrs. Hoover asked about the triangle, Allison said, "It's yellow like the little circles. It's a shape, too." She did what many young children do when they first begin to sort—she changed the sorting rule as she went along.

Carla and Paul were successfully able to sort the lids using different rules for their sorts. However, Paul did not believe that the lids could also be sorted by texture. He seemed to think they could be sorted by only one attribute (size), another misconception typical of young children. Later Mrs. Hoover went back to talk more with Carla and Paul. Carla showed Paul how she sorted by letting him touch the lids. Then Mrs. Hoover placed Paul's lids back into the bag and challenged him to sort his lids the way Carla had sorted hers. Hearing Carla's reasoning and being given the opportunity to re-sort his lids using her rule helped Paul understand that the same group of objects could be sorted in different ways.

When students sort, they naturally do so in quantitative ways. They count the number of objects in each group and compare these groups using language of *most*, *fewer*, and *equal*. "Informal comparing, classifying, and counting activities can provide the mathematical beginnings for developing young learners' understanding of data, analysis of data, and statistics" (NCTM 2000, 109).

In *The Young Child and Mathematics* (2000), Juanita V. Copley describes the levels of understanding young children progress through when learning to sort and classify. Her thinking may help clarify why children make sorting errors:

▶ At the first level, children take objects from a larger group based on a common attribute. They first focus on color and later notice shape, size, and texture. They may have difficulty explaining how objects have been sorted, and often do not apply a rule consistently.

▶ At the second level, children sort a collection of objects using a rule consistently. They often sort into two groups—for example, lids that are tall and lids that are not tall. "This two-part type of classification—*has* versus *has not*—is fundamental in collecting certain kinds of data (children who have cats and children who do not have cats) and in graphing and other representations of data" (155).

▶ At the third level, children sort and re-sort the same collection of objects. Children benefit from hearing how others sort and their reasoning.

▶ At the final level, children state a sorting rule and also state rules others have used to classify the same objects. Children recognize that the objects in the group have several common attributes and that the attributes are not shared by objects outside the group. They can determine whether a newly introduced object belongs inside or outside this group based on its attributes.

"The importance of sorting and classifying activities in children's mathematical development is critical. Through these activities children learn to think analytically and to express their thoughts clearly" (Baratta-Lorton 1995, 58).

Classifying is a necessary skill in many areas of mathematics. In order to recognize, duplicate, and extend patterns, students must be able to notice the attributes of the items in the pattern. In geometry, students sort shapes and create labels by identifying the number of sides or corners on a shape and later use the more formal vocabulary of vertices and edges. In measurement, they sort and classify objects by their overall size, length, weight, or volume. This exercise focuses students' thinking on the attribute that is being measured.

▪▪ *Ideas for Instruction*

The following activities will help children develop a foundation for understanding statistics:

▶ Have young students take part in cleaning up and reorganizing classroom materials. They can match materials with labeled shelves and alert you when quantities are low.

▶ Ask students to identify an object's attributes. For example, if students are exploring lids, ask them to choose their favorite lid and describe it. On another day, ask pairs of students to compare the lids they chose. Ask them to tell how their two lids are alike and how the lids are different.

▶ Provide a variety of materials for sorting and classifying. Begin with structured materials that have easily identifiable characteristics (teddy bear counters, pattern blocks, and so on).

▶ Have students explore attribute blocks, which include five shapes (circles, triangles, rectangles, squares, and hexagons) that vary by color (red, yellow, and blue), size (large and small), and thickness (thin and thick). The blocks are designed to develop flexible reasoning with regard to data characteristics. (Other suggestions for using attribute blocks are included in *Activities to Undo Math Misconceptions, Grades PreK–2*, page 109.)

▶ Gradually introduce unstructured materials (such as seashells, buttons, keys, or canceled postage stamps). Because these materials can be more difficult for children to describe and classify, scaffold the necessary language. (Classification tasks featuring buttons are included in *Activities to Undo Math Misconceptions, Grades PreK–2*, pages 110–112.)

▶ Allow children to decide on a sorting rule, which encourages them to use ideas they own and understand. Then have each child explain to the class how she or he sorted. Children benefit from hearing others' reasoning.

- Let children represent and sort data pictorially. For example, primary students might draw their favorite food served in the cafeteria. As a group, students then sort the food pictures into groups and tell what they notice about the data.

- Support children when they are sorting two- and three-dimensional shapes by encouraging them to describe how the shapes are alike and how they are different. This activity helps them appreciate shape definitions and create classes of shapes.

- Connect children's informal language to the more formal language used in organizing, describing, and analyzing data (for example, *all, some, not, equal, most, fewer, similar, in common, predict*).

▦ *Questions to Ponder*

1. What other instructional experiences help students develop their sorting and classifying concepts and skills?

2. What children's literature could be used to introduce sorting and classifying experiences? How?

▦ Choosing an Appropriate Display

When they want to display a specific set of data, many students assume they can choose randomly from a long list of different types. They don't recognize the specific purpose and varying qualities of bar graphs, line graphs, and line plots. The assumption that the displays are interchangeable leads to inaccurate graphical representations.

Also, once data have been collected and displayed, it needs to be analyzed. Interesting misconceptions abound as elementary students attempt to make sense of the graphs used to display their data. Students may focus on peripheral attributes of a graphic display when asked to interpret the data. Some students make inaccurate assumptions when comparing data displays based on visual differences such as a change in scale or a truncated axis. Students sometimes do not see how such attributes influence the appearance of the data, which leads to faulty interpretations.

Mr. Garner's students are exploring a connection between mathematics and science. Earlier, during a unit on plant growth, they planted seeds. Each group monitored and recorded the height of their plants weekly. One group's measurements are shown in Figure 5–2.

They now need to create a graph showing plant growth. The class has recently explored many types of data displays, and the walls of the classroom are filled with these representations. Student-made bar graphs show how each gets home in the afternoon. A line graph notes the change in the daily temperature for the month. Line plots reveal the number of siblings each student has. A pie chart displays the number of As, Bs, and Cs on a recent quiz.

For the plant growth data, students may either graph their own data or represent group data. Mr. Garner reviews the kinds of displays they have studied. He encourages them to look at the examples on the walls to help them decide which type of graph to make and then use the example of that kind of graph as a model. The students are eager to get started. They chat at their tables and begin gathering materials (graph paper, rulers, scissors, and markers).

Mr. Garner talks with students as they work. He asks Myrna about the line plot she has constructed (see Figure 5–3).

"Tell me about your data display, Myrna."

"I am making a line plot."

"What made you decide to use this type of graph?"

Figure 5–2 *Plant Growth Chart*

Plant Growth Chart

Week	Myrna	Victor	Angel	Ricardo
1	1 cm	2 cm	2 cm	1 cm
2	2 cm	3 cm	4 cm	3 cm
3	4 cm	5 cm	7 cm	6 cm
4	6 cm	7 cm	9 cm	8 cm
5	8 cm	9 cm	11 cm	9 cm

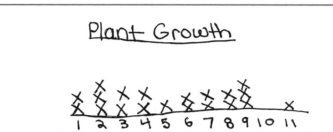

Figure 5–3 *Myrna's Line Plot*

"I am putting an X on the number line to show each height that the whole group measured for the five weeks."

"What will the line plot tell us about the growth of the plants?"

Myrna seems confused. She stops for a moment, tilts her head, and then says, "Let me finish it first and then I can tell you."

"Okay," Mr. Garner says, "I'll check back a little later."

He sits next to Victor and looks at Victor's graph (see Figure 5–4).

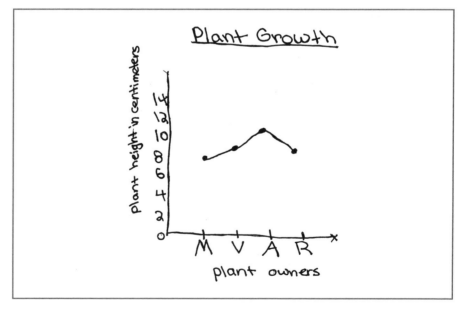

Figure 5–4 *Victor's Line Graph*

MATH MISCONCEPTIONS

"Victor, tell me about your graph."

"I made a line graph."

"What does it show?"

"It shows the difference between our plants *[pointing to the three other people in his group]* the last time we measured them."

"What made you choose a line graph?"

"Because I like the way they look when you connect the dots."

Mr. Garner prompts Victor to look at the sample line graphs around the room and mentions that a line graph should show change over time.

He knows he will need to begin tomorrow's lesson by reviewing the purpose of the different types of graphs.

▪▪ *Identifying the Error Pattern*

A couple of misconceptions led to Myrna's error in constructing her line plot. First, Mr. Garner did not specifically identify a data question, and Myrna felt compelled to show every piece of data on the growth table without first deciding the point of her display. She knew that a line plot was used to display numerical data rather than categorical data, and the plant heights were definitely numeric. Second, Myrna recognized that the values had a rather small range. Given that, she thought a number line (used to form a line plot) made sense. She looked at the data apart from the context, failing to see a purpose for the graph. Her graph shows the height of every group member's plant at five different points of time, which doesn't make sense. The values fit the parameters of a line plot, but the context does not. (Using a line plot to show the height of each classmate's plant at the end of a particular week would reveal trends in plant growth and be an appropriate application.)

Victor made a line graph. He knew that line graphs are used to show change over time, and he also knew that the height of the plants changed over time. He saw this as a perfect fit. His error came in the formation of the *x*-axis. Rather than showing the growth of a single plant over the five-week span, he displayed the final height of the plants for all four group members. Categorical data like this are best represented on a bar graph.

What the Research Says

Children are exposed to graphs in many ways, especially in newspapers and magazines, but it's important for them to collect, organize, analyze, and interpret data themselves. "Data analysis is about more than making graphs and calculating statistics" (Van de Walle 2007, 453). Data should be collected and displayed with a specific intent, not simply to graph data for the sake of making a graph. When students learn to formulate questions a graph is supposed to answer, they organize and display the data in a more meaningful way. They see the creation of the graph as one step in a bigger process of collecting data for a purpose. We want students to see a set of data as a whole to be described for a reason.

The *Principles and Standards for School Mathematics* states, "Students should become familiar with a variety of representations such as tables, line plots, bar graphs, and line graphs by creating them, watching their teacher create them, and observing those representations found in their environment" (NCTM 2000, 178). The selection of appropriate representations requires students to understand the difference between numerical data and categorical data. This classification process enables young learners to appropriately choose a specific display with a specific purpose.

Ideas for Instruction

▶ Make the data collection and analysis process meaningful by helping students first identify the question they wish to answer. Formulating the question provides direction in the collection and representation stages. Rather than graphing favorite ice cream flavors or class birthdays simply for the sake of making a graph, create a purposeful question the graph is meant to answer. Students will still learn the parts of a graph and how to put the pieces together, but with intent and purpose. Possible questions for elementary students include:

  ■ If we are buying ice cream for an upcoming celebration, which 3 flavors should we buy?

  ■ How will we know when someone in our class is celebrating a birthday?

  ■ How can we keep track of how everyone gets home from school in the afternoon?

  ■ What types of books should be purchased for the library?

  ■ Where in the room is the best place for our plants to grow?

▶ Provide examples of both numerical and categorical data so students will be more likely to understand why certain data displays are more appropriate than others.

- Numerical examples: age, shoe size, height, money earned
- Categorical examples: kinds of pets, movie types, foods, names

▶ Ask students to collect graphs from newspapers, magazines, and websites. Sort the examples according to types. Allow students to speculate why a specific graph was used to represent the data and why another representation would not work as well to convey the information.

▶ Create two different displays for a given set of data (perhaps a bar graph and a circle graph). Ask students to compare the two displays and discuss whether they carry the same message. This will help students see that the kind of graph they choose can impact the visual message. (One way to do this is by using connecting cubes to represent the bars on a bar graph. Students can then replicate the quantity of each color and arrange them in a circle to see how the same data would look as a circle graph. Children in the primary grades can do this activity, because it doesn't require understanding the degrees within a circle.)

▶ If students erroneously use a line graph to display and connect discrete pieces of data, ask them to name the value of any point along the line segment. Since a line graph plots change over time, all points of the line represent a value. If there are no values between the plotted points, the points should not be connected.

▶ Make large versions of graphs as a class (an easy way is to use a shower curtain liner and traffic tape). These visual aids enhance class discussions about the parts of a graph and the most appropriate way to display the data.

▶ Gather a collection of graph templates to which students can refer. These visual prompts can help students compare the potential final product and help connect the data to a potential display.

Questions to Ponder

1. How can you make the process of collecting and displaying data meaningful for your students?

2. What sorts of questions can your students answer by collecting data through surveys, observations, or experiments?

Understanding Terms for Measures of Central Tendency

Students often misunderstand the difference between mean, median, and mode. Their prior knowledge may lead them to ignore zero outcomes when finding the mean. When finding the mode, many students look for the highest score rather than the one with the greatest frequency. And many students fail to order data from least to most, thus creating an inaccurate median.

The *median* is the middle value of the data values listed, reordering the data from smallest to largest or vice versa. The *mode* means "the most" (not in terms of quantity of items, but in terms of the value that appears the most). The *mean* is the sum of all of the given numbers divided by the number of values, including zero as a value if it appears in the data.

It's the last day of a two-week study of mean, median, and mode in a fifth-grade classroom. To assess her students' overall understanding of these concepts, Ms. Reynolds gives them the Chocolate Chip Cookie Problem (see Figure 5–5).

Students work independently so Ms. Reynolds can evaluate them individually. No one seems particularly anxious as they settle down to work. After the papers have been handed in, Ms. Reynolds ends the period by asking students

---

How Many Chocolate Chips Are in Our Cookies?

Pretend you have each been given a chocolate chip cookie. The line plot below shows the number of chocolate chips each of these 26 cookies contains:

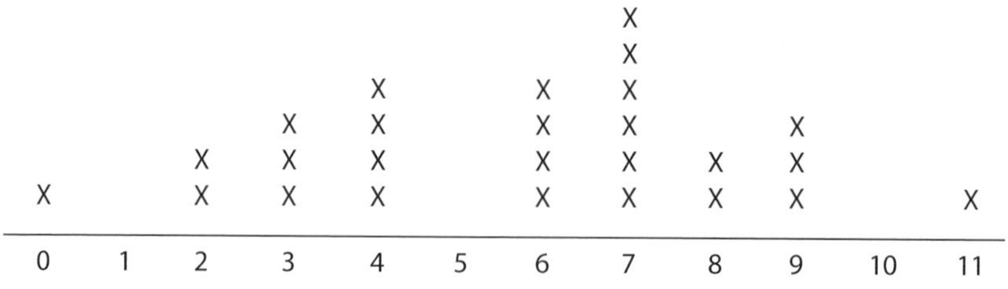

```
                                        X
                                        X
                        X           X   X
                    X   X           X   X           X
                X   X   X           X   X   X   X
        X       X   X   X           X   X   X   X               X
        _____
        0   1   2   3   4   5   6   7   8   9   10  11
```

Figure out the mean, median, and mode of the above data, and explain how you went about it.

Figure 5–5 *Chocolate Chip Cookie Problem*

what they particularly liked about this unit. From their comments, it's clear the students found conducting the experiments and surveys and displaying the results using different representations very engaging.

When she reads the students' papers, Ms. Reynolds discovers some very interesting misconceptions about what is meant by *mean, median,* and *mode.*

Catherine wrote, "11 is the mode because it's the amount of chocolate chips that is the most. And the mode is the most. The words even sound the same."

In figuring out the mean Marcus wrote, "The mean is 5.96 chocolate chips. I got this answer by adding up all of the amounts and then dividing by 25. I got 149 as the sum. If you divide that by 25 the answer is 5.96. That's almost 6 chocolate chips per cookie."

Brittany ordered her data in the following manner to determine the median:

7, 7, 7, 7, 7, 7, 6, 6, 6, 6, 4, 4, 4, 4, 9, 9, 9, 3, 3, 3, 8, 8, 2, 2, 11, 0

Then she wrote, "The median is 4. I put the numbers in order from the one that had the most chocolate chips (that was 7) to the one that had the fewest chocolate chips (that was a tie between the 11 and the 0). Then I counted from both ends to the middle of the list. There was an even amount of numbers. The two in the middle were both 4. So the median is 4."

▪▪ *Identifying the Misconceptions*

In order to remember which of these "averages" is which, students tend to oversimplify their definitions. If a teacher tells them that the word *mode* sounds just like its definition—*most*—students may remember the word but won't remember whether mode refers to the piece of data that represents the highest number (the "most") or the most frequently occurring number. That's what Catherine did. She explained that the mode referred to the amount that was the most—11.

Marcus did what so many students do when they are presented with a list of data that includes zero and asked to find the mean. He didn't include it either in the set of numbers he added together or in the divisor. Interestingly, it isn't only elementary and middle school students who have this misconception: "30 percent of preservice teachers said that adding zero to a set of data would not change the value of the mean" (Schwartz 1988, 41–52).

Students understand why the median is used to indicate the average of things like salaries or housing costs only if they have conducted experiments in which the logic of listing a set of number values in order from least to most and then determining the middle is made clear. And even though Brittany did this, she didn't list the number values from least to most or most to least but rather ranked the frequencies with which the number values appeared. Whatever the source of her confusion, her answer of 4 is incorrect; the median is 6.

What the Research Says

First, two discouraging findings:

▶ "Less than half the thirteen-year-olds in the United States are able to find the median of a set of data listed in order from least to greatest" (Carpenter et al. 1981). And when the data isn't listed in order or in a frequency table, student performance "may even be worse" (Zawojewski 2002).

▶ "A focused look at a traditional junior high school statistics topic—mean, median, and mode—indicates that students' performance may reflect a mastery of memorized procedures rather than a thorough understanding of the underlying concepts" (Zawojewski 2002, 238).

Now some suggestions:

▶ Statisticians typically think of the mean as the "point on a number line where the data on either side of the point are balanced" (Van de Walle 2007, 466). A line plot is a good way to present the data. Students can then picture the mean as a middle or balance point.

▶ "A balance beam where the mean acts as a fulcrum balancing a distribution of weights may help some students understand the concept" (Bright and Hoeffner 1993, 89).

▶ Elementary students should be exposed to the arithmetic average through concrete experiences in which they can discover the "add 'em up and then divide" rule (Zawojewski 2002).

▶ Students should be given the opportunity to develop their own definitions for mean, median, and mode based on the activities they experience.

▶ A variety of open-ended problems in which students are given the mean and then asked to create different data sets leading to this mean helps them make sense out of the averages they're finding.

▶ Asking students to answer real-world questions prompts them to make decisions about which statistic to use to best represent their data.

■■ *Ideas for Instruction*

▶ Whenever possible, link concrete experiences to the procedures students are using to determine mean, median, and mode. Here's one suggested activity (from *Activities to Undo Math Misconceptions, Grades 3–5*):

■ Each student first predicts the number of colored links he or she can connect in one minute and records these predictions on a line plot. Then each student takes a quantity of disconnected links, connects as many as she or he can in one minute, and adds these quantities to the original line plot in a different color in order to be able to compare predictions with the actual numbers.

■ Students then take their chains of colored links and arrange themselves in order, from the student with the shortest chain to the student with the longest chain. Students who have the same number of links stand behind each other. Tell students there's a name for the identical number of links connected by the most students—the *mode*, or the value that occurs most frequently in the data set.

■ Now determine the *median*, or "middle," quantity of colored links. Have students form one straight line, with no one behind anyone else. (Students with the same amount of links in their chain stand next to one another.) Ask students how they might figure out which person (that is, which chain) is in the exact middle of the line. No matter what's suggested ("folding the line in half," pairing the person who has the fewest links with the one who has the most), the median amount will easily be determined.

■ Next, tell students that it really isn't fair that someone was able to connect only 11 links while someone else connected 42. "We need to think of a fair way to share the colored links we've connected so everyone has about the same amount. There might be some left over, but we need each person in the class to have the same." During the "trading" that takes place, the concept of the *mean* becomes very real.

▶ Have students collect their own data—the shoe sizes of the students in the class, the ages of teachers in the school, attendance at home baseball games—and then determine the mean, median, and mode.

▶ Give students a variety of problems so they develop a truer sense of each measure of central tendency.

▶ Give students all the scores the class received on a test except one; also tell them the mean score. Ask them to determine what the missing score is and explain how they figured it out.

▶ Assign this problem: "The mean of five brothers' ages is 4, and the mode is 3. What are some possible ages for the five brothers?" (Van de Walle 2007, 239).

▶ To help students better understand the impact that zero has on determining the mean, have them construct different data sets for a specific mean where zero has to be included. Here's one such problem:

> Emily buys a large bag of candies. She eats some candy nearly every day for 2 weeks; her daily average is 12 candies. Create a data set showing specifically how many candies she eats on each day of the 2-week period. There must be at least 1 day where she doesn't eat any candy (from *Activities to Undo Math Misconceptions, Grades 3–5*).

▶ To help students make sense out of mean, have each student determine the length of his or her foot using cash register tape (Van de Walle 2007, 465). Tell them to write their name on their strip and the length in either inches or centimeters. Have students, in small groups of four or six, tape their "foot strips" end to end. Then ask them to come up with a method of finding the mean without using any of the lengths written on the strips. Have them share their methods with the entire class.

▦ *Questions to Ponder*

1. What other instructional experiences will allow students to better understand the meaning for mode, median, and mean?

2. What children's books could be used as a springboard for teaching mean, median, and mode? How?

⧉ Analyzing Data

A community organization has partnered with Riverdale Elementary School (grades 3–5) for a special nutrition initiative. The goal is to help students make smart snack choices. The community partnership will provide fruit snacks during lunch for several months. They ask the staff for advice about which fruits to serve, and the teachers jump on this practical opportunity to apply graphing and data analysis. Each grade level conducts a survey and creates a graph displaying their favorite fruit choices (see Figure 5–6).

Ms. Norbeck makes copies of all three graphs for her math students. She also makes a poster of each to display at the front of the room as a reference during class discussions.

"What do the data tell us about the fruit choices at our school?" Ms. Norbeck asks the class. For several minutes students review the data and discuss it in small groups. Then volunteers share their conclusions:

"Apples are the favorite in third grade."

"They are the favorite in fifth grade, too, but not in fourth."

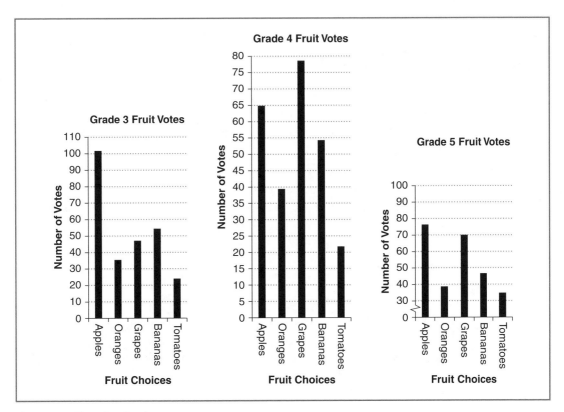

Figure 5–6 *Three Bar Graphs*

"Fourth grade loves grapes."

"I don't think we will be getting tomatoes."

Then Ms. Norbeck asks students to record their observations about the data.

Reviewing the student work later that day, she lists the student observations she needs to address the next day:

- "There are a whole lot of kids in fourth grade and hardly any kids in fifth grade." (Lillian)

- "Fourth grade likes bananas a lot more than third and fifth." (China)

- "Nobody likes tomatoes much, but fifth grade likes them the worst." (Camille)

- "Fifth grade voted for about twice as many apples as bananas." (Ryan)

■■ *Identifying the Error Pattern*

Lillian wrote that there were a whole lot of kids in fourth grade and not many in fifth grade, when in fact the number of students in each grade level was similar. She was equating the size of the bars with the sample size, not noticing that the third and fifth grades used a scale of ten, while the fourth grade used a scale of five. Additionally, the fifth grade y-axis is truncated—the zigzag line indicates that a segment has been removed: the scale begins at thirty.

China was also misled by the different scales when she stated that fourth graders liked bananas more than the other grades. The third and fourth grades had the same number of votes for bananas.

Camille and Ryan were confused by the truncated axis. Camille felt that fifth graders liked tomatoes less than any other grade, when tomatoes received more votes in fifth grade (33) than in fourth grade (22) and third grade (23). The truncated axis made the tomato bar look so much smaller than the other bars. Ryan was also fooled by the truncated axis when he said the number of votes for apples in fifth grade was about twice that for bananas. The bar for bananas may look to be about half the size of the bar for apples, but bananas received 46 votes and apples received 75 votes.

What the Research Says

"A big conceptual idea in data analysis can be referred to as the shape of data: a sense of how data are spread out or grouped, what characteristics about the data set as a whole can be described, and what the data tell us in a global way about the population from which they are taken" (Van de Walle 2007, 458). Data analysis allows students to formulate a response to the initial question being explored and requires them to reveal the nature or tendencies of the data in order to best explain the overall meaning. This process can be influenced by the types of graph used to communicate results.

We must teach students to compare and analyze data with a critical eye and teach them to look at the key attributes of a graph that influence the message portrayed. This activity requires meaningful practice through multiple experiences. "By providing students with examples of graphical displays to interpret, analyze, and construct, teachers can help students become alert to improper or misleading displays of data, whether intended or not" (Chapin and Johnson 2000, 213).

Principles and Standards for School Mathematics states that students should be able to select and use appropriate statistical methods to analyze data (NCTM 2000, 176). Included in this expectation is:

▶ Describing the shapes and important features of a set of data and comparing related data sets, with an emphasis on how the data are distributed

▶ Comparing different representations of the same data and evaluating how well each representation shows important aspects of the data

Being able to analyze graphical representations correctly allows students to make inferences or predictions based on the data. This is an important life skill that will enable them to make sense of the enormous amount of data they will encounter in the future.

Ideas for Instruction

▶ Use color to distinguish different categories of data on a graph (different-color connecting cubes or links when creating a graph with manipulatives, multicolored crayons or markers when constructing graphs on paper). Color variations allow students to more readily compare and contrast the data.

▶ Designate a space in the classroom in which to display a variety of tables and graphs. Encourage students to collect examples as well. Make a daily data chat part of the morning routine. Ask students to share what the data show, and brainstorm who might be interested in such information.

▶ Ask students to describe the shape of data—the visual image conveyed by a graph. Provide graphed data minus the titles and labels. Allow students to study the size of the bars (on bar graphs), the slope of the line (on line graphs), or the distribution of the Xs (on line plots). Ask students to describe the trends they see and name some possible titles and labels based on those trends. Or conduct this activity as a matching game: titles and labels on one set of cards, graphed data on another. Have students match the data to the correct title and labels.

Give students different-size representations of the same data. (Modifications might include changing the scale or the length of the axis.) Ask them to consider what is revealed by the different perspectives. Examples like these prompt rich discussions of comparisons and visual messages. For example, the two line graphs shown in Figure 5–7 include exactly the same information. However, at a glance one may erroneously conclude that the first graph shows data collected over a longer period of time. Or that the second shows a greater increase in the amount of money collected from year 2 to year 3. Helping students realize how choices with regard to the axes and the scales influence the appearance of the data will help learners be more critical in their data analysis.

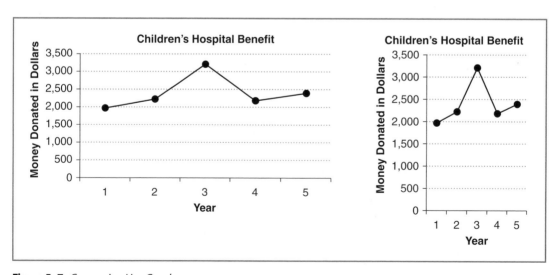

Figure 5–7 *Comparing Line Graphs*

► Use technology to expose students to multiple views of the same data. Many software applications allow students to input spreadsheet quantities and then choose from a variety of displays. With the click of the mouse, students can see the data transformed from a bar graph to a circle graph (see Figure 5–8).

By comparing the data as represented on different types of graphs, students can decide which provides a clearer picture of their intent. If students choose an incorrect display (for example, turn the pie chart above into the line graph shown in Figure 5–9) you can ask about the validity of the data and the appropriateness of the graph given the data set.

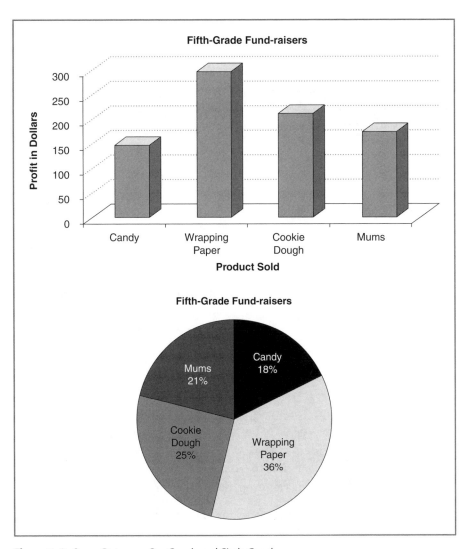

Figure 5–8 *Same Data on a Bar Graph and Circle Graph*

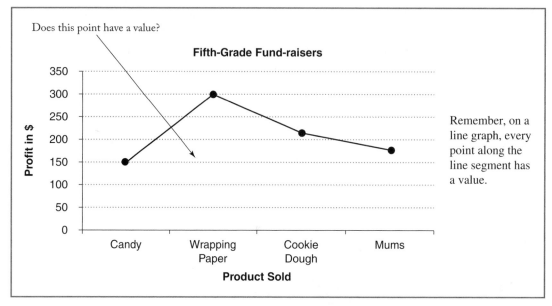

Figure 5–9 *Data Incorrectly Displayed as a Line Graph*

:: *Questions to Ponder*

1. What are some authentic opportunities for data collection, display, and analysis in your classroom?

2. What kinds of data questions would be of interest to your students?

Probability

Mr. Stevens's fourth graders are experimenting with number generators. He asks what it means for a game to be "fair." Alonso says that a game is fair if all of the players have the same chance to win. Carmen adds that games that are fair are fun to play. Melanie says that games are fair when no player will win more often than another player, even though there is some chance involved.

Mr. Stevens is pleased with the discussion and gives the students the following problem (see Figure 5–10 from *Activities to Undo Math Misconceptions, Grades 3–5*):

Name _____ Date _____

What Makes a Game Fair?

Before beginning this activity decide who will be Player 1 and who will be Player 2.

Player 1: _____

Player 2: _____

You have two decahedron die that will be tossed. Player 1 gets a point if the *product* of the 2 die is **even**. Player 2 gets a point if the *product* of the 2 die is **odd**. Talk about whether you think this will be a "fair" game given these directions. Explain in writing what makes this fair or unfair.

_____

_____

_____

_____

_____

_____

_____

_____

_____

_____

Then, decide on a way to keep track of your tosses and do this experiment for 25 tosses. Look at your data and compare what you thought would happen with what actually happened.

Be prepared to share your observations and your ideas about what happened.

Figure 5–10 *What Makes a Game Fair?*

Each pair of students decides how they will collect and represent the data. Some students write "even" or "odd," some write the product for each toss, others write out the entire equation.

As things begin to wind down, Mr. Stevens tells the students to look over their data and be prepared to share the results with the class. Not one pair has more odd products than even. In some cases the even products outnumber the odd products overwhelmingly. One pair has 20 even products and only 5 odd products. Students seem surprised by this. "We got 18 even products and only 7 odd products," Jamara says. "Way more than half of the time an even product happened."

Mr. Stevens asks the pairs that kept track of the entire equation to share some of the even products and some of the odd products. He records these on the board in two separate columns, asking students to look for patterns. One student says that every time there is an odd product the two factors are both odd numbers, but no one seems to find this terribly important. Mr. Stevens asks what sorts of numbers appear in the equations when an even product is obtained. Students observe that the factors are either both even or even and odd.

Next Mr. Stevens asks who won each contest and tallies the results under the headings *Player 1* and *Player 2*. Player 1 has won every time. He then asks table groups to discuss whether this was a fair game and why or why not.

After five minutes he calls on one student from each table to share. In *every* case students say they decided the game is fair, because there is an equal amount of even and odd digits on each die. No one uses the data collected to change the original prediction.

▀▀ *Identifying the Error Pattern*

Why couldn't these students use their earlier discussions and the data on the board to conclude that the game was not fair? Two even factors create an even product, but so does an odd factor and an even factor. The only way to produce an odd product is with two odd factors. Why couldn't students see that the even products outnumbered the odd products 3 to 1?

Most likely several things came into play:

▶ Mr. Stevens might not have spent time with the students looking at the patterns that occur when numbers are multiplied together. If he didn't, the students wouldn't know how to use this sort of evidence to find answers to problems.

▶ They might also not be aware that the larger the data sample, the more useful the data. Small sample sizes (25 tosses, or even 50 tosses) might lead students to believe that the element of chance created the outcomes they were seeing. Had they looked carefully at the entire class' data and tried to make sense of it, they should have realized that the sample size was now quite large (12 pairs times 25 tosses equals 300 outcomes with only 78 being odd). A sample size this large and data this skewed would suggest that Player 1 always has the better chance of winning.

▶ It's difficult for students, even fourth-graders, to change their minds. Believing that the number of even and odd digits on each die made the game fair, it was hard to concede that this didn't matter. They focused on an attribute they believed impacted the fairness of the game, and they couldn't shift their focus to other attributes.

What the Research Says

NCTM's *Focal Points* (2006) includes nothing about introducing the idea of probability in the elementary classroom. Probability isn't mentioned as part of the curriculum until seventh grade, and then it's not even a focal point but only a "connection to the focal points." This doesn't mean we shouldn't provide students with opportunities to use a spinner, dice, coins, and other materials in experiments and games, but it might mean that in an activity like the one in Mr. Stevens' class the emphasis should be more on noticing patterns—looking at factors and products—and not on whether the activity is fair or unfair.

In a study conducted with eleven-year-olds, researchers noted a "negative tendency effect" in connection with the following problem: "A fair coin is flipped four times, each time landing with heads up: HHHH. What is the most likely outcome if the coin is flipped a fifth time? Please circle one of the answers. (A) a head (B) a tail (C) a head and a tail are equally likely." Many students circled B, their reasoning being that because the coin had landed on heads so many times it was more likely that a tail would occur next (Ryan and Williams 2007, 129–30). The logic behind this is unsound, based on what the students think ought to happen rather than the theoretical probability of what will happen. Perhaps, as Hoemann and Ross point out in their 1982 survey, educators of adolescents should be looking for strategies to help them learn about probability.

Ideas for Instruction

▶ Give children in prekindergarten and kindergarten simple spinners with half the face colored red and the other half colored blue. Ask them to predict which color will be landed on most often. Then let them spin and keep track of what happens. Talking about how many times red or blue is landed on lets them see there is an equally likely chance of red or blue, since each has the same amount of space on the spinner. Then have them make spinners with larger or smaller amounts of red and blue, and perhaps a third color, and let them test out their predictions. A good kindergarten activity is to split a spinner into three parts, half colored blue, a fourth colored red, and a fourth colored yellow (see *Activities to Undo Math Misconceptions, Grades PreK–2*).

▶ Give young children a real-life introduction to random packaging. Give each child a small ("fun-sized") package of candies (approximately 16–23 pieces). List the colors the candies inside might be. Then ask them to predict which color pieces their package will have the most of. Capture this information in a graph and have students open their packages, sort their candies, and represent each color in a row or column. (It's likely some children won't have any candies of a specific color. They may see this as "unfair," which is a great segue for you to discuss how arbitrary fairness can be.)

▶ Talk about probability as it pertains to life. Discuss the weather report and how meteorologists discuss the likelihood of precipitation. Keep track of the weather for a month and have students talk about the type of weather that is likely to occur every year at this same time. Talk about the seasons, making a connection between science, social studies, measurement, probability, and the type of weather that is possible in various places across the United States or the world.

▶ Read the book *Cloudy with a Chance of Meatballs*, by Judi Barrett (1978), and discuss the probability that the sky will rain meatballs. Children could even write their own page for a book about things that are unlikely to happen.

▶ Use colored cubes in bags to introduce probability vocabulary. Place 10 cubes inside an opaque bag—5 yellow cubes, 4 red cubes, and 1 green cube. Ask students whether it's possible to put your hand inside and pull out a red cube, green cube, or yellow cube. Ask whether it's more probable that one color will be picked than another and why. Ask whether they think it's possible to pull out a blue cube. (Don't be surprised if some students say that it's possible!) Then give each pair of students a bag with these cubes inside and have them put their hand in, pull out a cube, record its color, and put it back inside. Have partners take turns for a total of 20 reach-in-and-pull-outs and record the data. Discuss the results to see whether the full class' data are similar to what happened to pairs (from *Activities to Undo Math Misconceptions, Grades PreK–2*).

▶ Have intermediate students practice computational fluency while they collect data from probability experiments. Ask students to determine all the possible sums (36) that can be tossed with 2 six-sided dice. Then ask them to predict which sum will come up most often and why they think so. Have each student toss the dice as many times as possible (given a specific amount of time), record these sums, and capture the data in an individual line plot. As students share their results, ask whether there were certain sums that seemed to come up most frequently. Wonder aloud why this might be. Ask students how likely it is for a sum of 2 to come up. (You don't want numerical probability but rather a general term like *highly unlikely*, which is a fair way to assess the likelihood that the sum of 2 or 12 will appear when tossing 2 six-sided dice.) Older students can be asked to find the fraction that represents the frequency that each sum could appear. (See *Activities to Undo Math Misconceptions, Grades 3–5*.)

▶ Engage and motivate older students by connecting probability to physical activities. Have them determine their longest running broad jump and their longest standing broad jump and then compare these distances with those achieved by other students. Have them develop a double bar graph depicting the relationship between a person's height and the length they've jumped.

Few of these concepts and skills will be included on either state or national assessments. That doesn't mean that students shouldn't be exposed to the ideas surrounding probability. These activities are also opportunities for them to practice and reinforce other mathematics skills.

▪▪ *Questions to Ponder*

1. What sorts of social studies, science, or language arts activities could be combined with probability and data collecting so that students see these activities as meaningful and useful?

2. How might you use probability activities to assess students' fluency with basic facts (addition or multiplication)?

6 Assessing Children's Mathematical Progress

J ust as it's important to recognize students' misconceptions, it's important to know their thinking about all the mathematics they are learning, so we can better support them as they make sense of these concepts and skills. When we encourage students to share their problem-solving strategies and explain their thinking about a mathematical concept, we learn important information about what they understand.

▣ Assessment: The Received View

Traditionally, mathematics assessments are summative and focus on computation procedures—a student's ability to complete a procedure. Without an oral or written explanation (as is often the case with selected response items), it's difficult to analyze a student's understanding or lack thereof. Therefore, educators receive an incomplete picture of what a student knows and can do.

Most standardized "benchmark" assessments also emphasize low-level procedural skills, and many teachers feel pressured to revert to drill and practice in order to meet districtwide goals. Conceptual understanding is difficult to measure in a standardized format, so explanations of strategies and processes aren't asked for—and if it's not being assessed, teachers may feel there's no need to spend time teaching this way. As they prepare students for statewide assessments (often from early January until the assessments are given), the problem-based tasks that enhance students' understanding of mathematics and their ability to apply mathematics skills are often eliminated from the instructional day. Teachers often feel there just isn't time to do both.

Standardized assessments provide only one piece of information about what a child knows and can do. That information should never be viewed in isolation when considering a child's instructional plan. "Assessment should not merely be done *to* students; rather, it should also be done *for* students, to guide and enhance their learning" (NCTM 2000, 22).

"Recognizing that public demands for accountability, and consequently for standardized tests, are not likely to disappear in the near future, some states are customizing the development of standardized tests that more closely align with both the content and the pedagogy implicit in the NCTM *Curriculum and Evaluation Standards*" (Stenmark 1991, 9). This is certainly an important and encouraging step.

▣ Assessment from a Better Angle

Formative assessment is an ongoing process that informs and directs the decisions we make about instruction for all our students. Paper-and-pencil tasks may be part of this process, but information is also gathered from students' answers to the questions we ask during a lesson, the observations we make as students work to solve problems, and the writing we collect when we ask students to explain how they got their answers. Assessment like this doesn't look different from instruction; rather, it is a big part of instruction.

Our goal must be to continually seek information about our students' mathematical thinking by using a variety of formative assessments. By keeping a record of what we've seen and heard, we form a more accurate picture of what our students know and can do. Misconceptions in the way students are thinking about a concept will become evident in their explanations. Error patterns often surface when students share representations of their problem solving.

Formative assessments take place while students are meaningfully engaged in doing and talking about mathematics. They may include interviews, math journals, evidence of students' self-monitoring, the results of performance tasks, or observations. Opportunities for formative assessment abound in our daily discussions with students. In order to take advantage of these opportunities, we must have a solid understanding of the mathematics concepts and skills being taught in order to know why an error has occurred and what can be done to improve understanding.

In the vignettes and student dialogues throughout this book, students' misconceptions and error patterns are evident as they grapple with challenging problems. In most of these classrooms getting the answer is not the only goal. Teachers use questions to probe for understanding and uncover error patterns. Problem-solving experiences allow students to think more deeply about mathematics and give the teacher a clearer sense of the source of such errors.

▣ Types of Formative Assessments

▦ *Student Discussions*

Listening to students during their discussions is an important way to determine any misconceptions they may have and diagnose their error patterns. The dialogues in this book model ways to assess student thinking about a particular concept or skill: teachers routinely asked students to explain their thinking or tell what they knew or whether a strategy that helped them solve a particular problem was efficient.

Sometimes students' solutions are correct, but their reasoning in reaching them is flawed. Unless students explain their thinking, a misconception may never be revealed. The questions we ask our students give us the information we need to redirect their thinking. If we observe that many students have the same misunderstanding, we need to reflect on how we taught the skill or concept, and then rethink what we did or said. Teachers play a big role in facilitating student discussions by asking questions and making mental or written records of what's being shared.

▦ *Partner or Small-Group Work*

Small-group or paired tasks give teachers many opportunities to observe students informally as they work on a problem. We can record our observations on index cards or address labels and ask probing questions to gather additional information. At any grade level, centers offer many opportunities to observe and assess students. Since the tasks are often completed without our direction, we can step back and note strategies used to get answers as well as observe how easily a task is completed.

▦ *Written Responses*

Students' written responses provide the clearest evidence of misconceptions or errors. If a student records the sum of 15 and 76 as 811, we know the answer is incorrect and can infer the reasoning behind the error. It's through the student's written explanation that we get an insight into how the misconception developed or where the error occurred.

In a community of learners, student writing about the strategies they've used can be shared with peers and they can work together to respectfully address errors. Encouraging the rest of the class to test a strategy we recognize as flawed may help the student who used the strategy to recognize the errors it contains.

■■ Representations

Students' representations can be concrete, pictorial, or symbolic. They reveal how students are organizing and communicating their thinking and reasoning. Collecting and analyzing students' representations gives us information about their understandings, misconceptions, and error patterns. These representations also provide support for conversations with parents about how their child is progressing.

■■ Diagnostic Interviews

A one-on-one diagnostic interview is an effective method for gathering data about a student's abilities and identifying the strategies he or she used to solve a problem. The student has an opportunity to convey verbally his or her thinking about a specific mathematics concept or skill. You can allow more "wait time" than in a typical lesson, giving the student a chance to formulate an explanation, which can be critical in diagnosing misconceptions or error patterns.

These interviews can be time consuming. But, by planning your questions and thinking about possible responses, you can conduct a diagnostic interview in as little as five minutes. A diagnostic interview is not a time to teach; it is a time to observe and listen to what a student knows and can do. Thank the student for participating, and record your notes on the interview afterward. Children are masters at reading our reactions, so it's important that they feel good about the experience.

■■ Open-Ended Questioning

Open-ended questions or prompts provide additional opportunities for children to show what they know in a variety of ways. Open-ended questions, questions posed in such a way that a variety of responses or strategies to get answers are possible, encourage students to think more critically and creatively. They also reveal any misconceptions a child may have about a mathematical concept or skill. By simply asking students to explain, either orally or in writing, how they figured out an answer, important information about what they understood in their problem solving emerges.

Open-ended questions also allow most students the opportunity to contribute because they can be answered in a variety of ways. "What's an observation you can make about today's graph?" allows for many responses, compared with, "Which color do most people in our class like the best?" An open-ended computation question might be, "How might you find the difference between 543 and 198?"

Consider the many different responses that could be given to such a prompt. In contrast, the question, "What's the difference between 543 and 198?" allows for only one answer and would likely reveal little about student thinking.

Questions or prompts that we have found to be effective when facilitating student discussions include:

- How did you figure out your answer?

- Did someone else get this same answer using a different strategy?

- What would happen if you...?

- What do you know about...?

- How did you know that this strategy would work?

- What did you find out when you...?

- Will someone explain what _____ said using your own words?

- Did you change your mind? Tell how you are thinking about this problem now.

- Will this work if we try it with other numbers/shapes?

We've found that assessments that are open-ended provide teachers with so much information about a student's level of understanding. If students are all given this activity, "The answer is 24. What is the question?" the detail of the response provides the teacher with far more information than the response to a story problem or expression. A second-grade student might write, "What is the sum of 18 and 6?" While another could write, "Margarette saved 3 dimes each week from her allowance. At the end of 8 weeks how many dimes will she have? How much money will she have saved?" The exciting thing about open-ended activities is that this same question could be used in a fifth-grade classroom. And a variety of responses would be expected from fifth graders as well. Examples of open-ended activities might include:

- 2 is the quotient of some expression. What is the expression?

- Use base-ten blocks to represent a number greater than 206.

- What example can you show to highlight the relationships that exist among the radius, diameter, and circumference of a circle?

- The height of a rectangle is 7 cm. What is the size of the base? And what is the perimeter?

- What are some differences between a square and a pentagon?

- What are some odd/even numbers greater than 29?

Constructed-Response Questions

A constructed-response question requires students to apply what they know about a mathematics concept or skill to explain why a solution makes sense. For example, you might first ask students to identify an appropriate unit of measure to estimate the length of an object, then ask them to explain (using words, numbers, or pictures) why that unit of measure makes sense. The explanation provides valuable information about what students know about the concept of units of measure. Many states use brief constructed-response items on the assessments they give to third through eighth graders. These items are then scored on a rubric based on specific criteria. Feedback to students through that rubric score provides students with important information regarding their own performance and next steps for learning.

Performance Tasks

Performance tasks are generally project-based, involve active student participation, require more student thinking and reasoning than a typical assessment, and can take more than one class period. Administering performance tasks to pairs or small groups of students also lets you observe how well they collaborate. Manipulative materials are often provided in connection with a performance task, so students can use them to think about how to solve the problem. An example of a performance task is asking fifth graders to collect data about the television preferences of students in the school, display and analyze the data, and interpret their potential application.

Closure Discussions

In a busy day of instruction, this critical time, in which students share what they have learned during a lesson, is sometimes forgotten or eliminated. By facilitating this discussion we find out what students think the lesson was about and what they learned. Misconceptions often come to light during a closure discussion and can be clarified either immediately or the next day.

▪▪ *Exit Cards or Exit Tickets*

In this strategy, we ask students, individually, to complete an exit card or exit ticket on which they tell us what they learned from a lesson or explain an idea or relationship on which a lesson was based.

Some "exit tickets" might be:

- Use connecting cubes to model and then determine the sum of 47 and 26. Explain what you did to get your answer.

- Represent, in four different ways, how to split a 4-centimeter square into halves.

- Use the array model, on a grid, to represent all factors of 24.

- Figure out what time you would need to wake up to catch the bus at 8:10 a.m. if it takes you 15 minutes to get dressed, 10 minutes to wash up, and 20 minutes to eat breakfast. Show all of your work.

▪▪ *Student Portfolios*

A portfolio is a folder of student work, collected throughout the year, that demonstrates a student's progress in, understanding of, and attitudes toward the mathematics he or she is learning. It's more comprehensive than any single assessment. An essential component is our discussion and reflection (orally or in writing) with the student about her or his strengths, areas for improvements, and attitudes toward mathematics. Many teachers encourage students to select some of their work to be put into their portfolio. Students are also encouraged to take their portfolios home and share them with their families.

▣ Why Assess?

The information we collect about our students' learning should be from a variety of sources and be useful in making instructional decisions. Embedding informal observations and formative assessments into our daily teaching makes our instruction much more effective and makes summative assessment far less time consuming.

In the classroom scenarios described in this book, students are generally comfortable representing, discussing, or writing about their thinking related to mathematical problem solving. This type of learning environment allows us to more easily implement informal observations and formative assessments and recognize how such opportunities drive instruction. Asking students to reflect on their reasoning and thinking during student discussions:

- Provides important information about misconceptions or error patterns

- Allows students to benefit from the thinking of their classmates

- Allows students to evaluate their own thinking

Children also need to understand their progress, and specific feedback from us, communicated in a positive way, is vital. Learning is greatly affected by timely and effective feedback to students.

▣ Final Thoughts

Assessment must become an integral and ongoing part of our mathematics instruction so that we are better able to monitor our students' growth and make decisions that will affect learning in positive ways. Often, the most effective assessments are conducted informally.

Student discussions are daily opportunities to monitor children's development as mathematical thinkers. Students' written responses and representations present evidence of how they are thinking and can be shared with families. Varied types of assessments provide a more thorough evaluation of a child's progress with the concepts and skills being taught and allow us to identify error patterns and correct misconceptions. And we cannot overlook the importance of having students monitor their own learning and consider the thinking and strategies of others. Students who have these kinds of experiences are more likely to own their learning and become empowered mathematicians.

References

Anghileri, J., and D. C. Johnson. 1988. "Arithmetic Operations on Whole Numbers: Multiplication and Division." In *Teaching Mathematics in Grades K–8: Research Based Methods*, edited by T. R. Post, 146–89. Boston: Allyn & Bacon.

Ashlock, Robert B. 1994. *Error Patterns in Computation*. New York: Macmillan.

Baek, Jae-Meen. 1998. "Children's Invented Algorithms for Multidigit Multiplication Problems." In *The Teaching and Learning of Algorithms in School Mathematics*, edited by L. Morrow and M. Kenney, 151–60. Reston, VA: National Council of Teachers of Mathematics.

Baratta-Lorton, Mary. 1995. *Mathematics Their Way*. Parsippany, NJ: Addison-Wesley.

Baroody, Arthur J. 1990. "How and When Should Place-Value Concepts and Skills Be Taught?" *Journal for Research in Mathematics Education* 21 (4): 282–86.

Baroody, Arthur J., and Dorothy J. Standifer. 1993. "Addition and Subtraction in Primary Grades." In *Research Ideas for the Classroom: Early Childhood Mathematics*, edited by Robert J. Jensen, 92–102. Reston, VA: National Council of Teachers of Mathematics.

Bezuk, N. S., and M. Bieck. 1993. "Current Research on Ration Numbers and Common Fractions: Summary and Implications for Teachers." In *Research Ideas for the Classroom: Middle Grade Mathematics*, edited by D. T. Owens, 118–36. National Council of Teachers of Mathematics Research Interpretation Project. New York: Macmillan.

Billstein, Rick, Shlomo Libeskind, and Johnny Lott. 2007. *A Problem Solving Approach to Mathematics for Elementary School Teachers*, 7th edition. Boston: Pearson Education.

Booth, Lesley R. 1984. *Algebra: Children's Strategies and Errors*. Windsor, England: NFER-Nelson.

Bright, George W., and Karl Hoeffner. 1993. "Measurement, Probability, Statistics, and Graphing." In *Research Ideas for the Classroom: Middle Grades Mathematics*, edited by Douglas T. Owens. Reston, VA: National Council of Teachers of Mathematics.

Burger, William F., and J. Michael Shaughnessy. 1986. "Characterizing the van Hiele Levels of Development in Geometry." *Journal for Research in Mathematics Education* 17 (January): 31–48.

Burns, Marilyn. 2000. *About Teaching Mathematics*. Sausalito, CA: Math Solutions.

Campbell, Patricia F., Thomas E. Rowan, and Anna R. Suarez. 1998. "What Criteria for Student-Invented Algorithms?" In *The Teaching and Learning of Algorithms in School Mathematics*, edited by L. Morrow and M. Kenney, 49–55. Reston, VA: National Council of Teachers of Mathematics.

Carle, Eric. 1972. *Rooster's Off to See the World*. New York: Aladdin.

Carpenter, Thomas P., Deborah A. Carey, and Vicky L. Kouba. 1990. "A Problem-Solving Approach to the Operations." In *Mathematics for the Young Child*, edited by Joseph Payne. Reston, VA: National Council of Teachers of Mathematics.

Carpenter, Thomas P., Mary Kay Corbitt, Henry S. Kepner, Mary Montgomery Lindquist, and Robert E. Reys. 1981. *Results from the Second Mathematics Assessment of the National Assessment of Educational Progress*. Reston, VA: National Council of Teachers of Mathematics.

Carpenter, Thomas P., and James M. Moser. 1983. "The Acquisition of Addition and Subtraction Concepts." In *Acquisition of Mathematics Concepts and Processes*, edited by Richard Lesh and Marsha Landau. New York: Academic Press.

Carroll, William M., and Denise Porter. 1997. "Invented Strategies Can Develop Meaningful Mathematical Procedures." *Teaching Children Mathematics* 3 (March): 370–74.

Chapin, Suzanne H., and Art Johnson. 2000. *Math Matters Grades K–6: Understanding the Math You Teach*. Sausalito, CA: Math Solutions.

Clements, Douglas H., and Julie Sarama (Eds.). 2004. *Engaging Young Children in Mathematics—Standards for Early Childhood Mathematics Education*. Mahwah, NJ: Lawrence Erlbaum.

Clements, Douglas H., and Michael T. Battista. 1992. "Geometry and Spatial Reasoning." In *Handbook of Research on Mathematics Teaching and Learning*, edited by Douglas A. Grouws, 420–64. New York: Macmillan, and Reston, VA: National Council of Teachers of Mathematics.

Cobb, Paul, and Grayson Wheatley. 1988. "Children's Initial Understandings of Ten." *Focus on Learning Problems in Mathematics* 10 (3): 1–28.

Copley, Juanita V. 2000. *The Young Child and Mathematics*. Reston, VA: National Council of Teachers of Mathematics.

Doig, B., J. Williams, L. Wo, and M. Pampaka. 2006. "Integrating Errors into Developmental Assessment: 'Time' for Ages 8–13." *Proceedings of the 30th Conference of the International Group for the Psychology of Mathematics Education* (2): 441–48. Prague: Charles University.

Drum, Randall L., and W. G. Petty, Jr. 1999. "Teaching the Values of Coins." *Teaching Children Mathematics*. Reston, VA: National Council of Teachers of Mathematics.

Ennis, Bonnie H., and K. S. Witeck. 2007. *Introduction to Representation, Grades 3–5*. Portsmouth, NH: Heinemann.

Falkner, K. P., L. Levi, and Thomas P. Carpenter. 1999. "Children's Understanding of Equality: A Foundation for Algebra." *Teaching Children Mathematics* (December): 232–36.

Fennell, Francis (Skip), Honi J. Bamberger, Thomas E. Rowan, Kay B. Sammons, and Anna R. Suarez. 2000. *Connect to Standards 2000: Making the Standards Work at Grade 2*. Chicago: Creative Publications.

Fuys, David J., and Amy K. Liebov. 1993. "Geometry and Spatial Sense." In *Research Ideas for the Classroom: Early Childhood Mathematics*, edited by Robert J. Jeson, 195–222. Reston, VA: National Council of Teachers of Mathematics.

Gelman, R., and C. R. Gallistel. 1986. *The Child's Understanding of Number*. London: Harvard University Press.

Giganti, Paul. 1994. *How Many Snails? A Counting Book*. New York: Harper Trophy.

Graeber, Anna O., and Patricia F. Campbell. 1993. "Misconceptions About Multiplication and Division." *Arithmetic Teacher* 40 (March): 408–11.

Haycock, D. 2001. *Mathematics Explained for Primary Teachers*. 2d ed. London: Paul Chapman Publishing.

Haycock, D., and A. Cockburn. 1997. *Understanding Mathematics in the Lower Primary Years*. London: Paul Chapman Publishing.

Hershkowitz, Rina, and Zvia Markovits. 2002. "Conquer Mathematics Concepts by Developing Visual Thinking." In *Putting Research into Practice in the Elementary Grades: Readings from Journals of the National Council of Teachers of Mathematics*, edited by Donald L. Chambers, 168–73. Reston, VA: National Council of Teachers of Mathematics.

Hiebert, James. 1984. "Why Do Some Children Have Trouble Learning Measurement Concepts?" *The Arithmetic Teacher* 31 (March): 19–24.

Hoemann, H. W., and B. M. Ross. 1982. "Children's Concepts of Chance and Probability." In *Children's Logical and Mathematical Cognition*, edited by C. J. Brainerd, 93–121. New York: Springer-Verlag.

Hoffer, Alan R. 1977. *Mathematics Resource Project: Geometry and Visualization*. Palo Alto, CA: Creative Publications.

Hughes, M. 1986. *Children and Number: Difficulties in Learning Mathematics*. Oxford: Blackwell.

Irons, Rosemary R., and Carmel Diezmann. 2008. *Space and Shape*. UK/Australia: ORIGO Education.

Kamii, Constance. 2006. "Measurement of Length: How Can We Teach It Better?" *Teaching Children Mathematics*. Reston, VA: National Council of Teachers of Mathematics.

Kuchemann, Dietmar. 1981. "Algebra." In *Children's Understanding of Mathematics: 11–16*, edited by K. M. Hart, 102–19. London: John Murray.

Lawton, Fiona. 2005. In *Children's Errors in Mathematics: Understanding Common Misconceptions in Primary Schools*, edited by Alice Hansen. Exeter, UK: Learning Matters Ltd.

Leibeck, P. 1984. *How Children Learn Mathematics*. London: Penguin Books.

Ma, Liping. 1999. *Knowing and Teaching Elementary Mathematics*. Mahwah, NJ: Lawrence Erlbaum.

Nagda, Ann Whitehead, and Cindy Bickel. 2000. *Tiger Math*. New York: Henry Holt.

National Mathematics Advisory Panel. 2008. *Foundations for Success: The Final Report of the National Mathematics Advisory Panel*. Washington D.C.: U.S. Department of Education.

National Council of Teachers of Mathematics. 1993. *Assessment in the Mathematics Classroom*, edited by Norman L. Webb and Arthur F. Coxford. Reston, VA: National Council of Teachers of Mathematics.

———. 2000. *Principles and Standards for School Mathematics*. Reston, VA: National Council of Teachers of Mathematics.

———. 2006. *Curriculum Focal Points for Prekindergarten Through Grade 8 Mathematics: A Quest for Coherence*. Reston, VA: National Council of Teachers of Mathematics.

New Zealand Council for Educational Research. 2008. *Algebraic Thinking, 1–3*. Assessment Resource Banks.

Nichols, Eugene D., and Sharon L. Schwartz. 1993. *Mathematics Dictionary and Handbook*. Honesdale, PA: Nichols Schwartz.

O'Connell, S. 2007. *Introduction to Problem Solving: Grades 3–5.* Portsmouth, NH: Heinemann.

Richardson, Kathy. 1984. *Developing Number Concepts Using Unifix Cubes*, Parsipanny, NJ: Addison-Wesley.

———. 1999. *Developing Number Concepts: Place Value, Multiplication, and Division.* Parsippany, NJ: Dale Seymour.

Ryan, Julie, and Julian Williams. 2007. *Children's Mathematics 4–15: Learning from Errors and Misconceptions.* New York: Open University Press.

Schwartz, Judah. 1988. "Intensive Quantity and Referent Transforming Arithmetic Operations." In *Number Concepts and Operations in the Middle Grades*, edited by J. Hiebert and M. Behr, 41–52. Hillsdale, NJ: Erlbaum.

Sherman, H. S., L. Richardson, and G. J. Yard. 2005. *Teaching Children Who Struggle with Mathematics—A Systematic Approach to Analysis and Correction.* Upper Saddle River, NJ: Pearson Education.

Silver, Edward A., Lora J. Shapiro, and Adam Deutsch. 1993. "Sense Making and the Solution of Division Problems Involving Remainders: A Examination of Middle School Students' Solutions Processes and Their Interpretations of Solutions." *Journal for Research in Mathematics Education* 24 (March): 117–35.

Stavy, Ruth, and Dina Tirosh. 2000. *How Students (Mis-)Understand Science and Mathematics.* New York: Teachers College Press.

Steen, Lynn Arthur. 1988. "The Science of Patterns." *Science* 240 (29 April): 611–16.

Stenmark, Jean Kerr (Ed.). 1991. *Mathematics Assessment: Myths, Models, Good Questions, and Practical Suggestions.* Reston, VA: National Council of Teachers of Mathematics.

Tennyson, R. D., J. Youngers, and P. Suebsonthi. 1983. "Concept Learning of Children Using Instructional Presenting Forms for Prototype Formation and Classification-Skill Development." *Journal of Education Psychology* 75: 280–91.

Thompson, C. S. 1990. "Place Value and Larger Numbers." In *Mathematics for the Young Child*, edited by J. N. Payne, 89–108. Reston, VA: National Council of Teachers of Mathematics.

Usiskin, Zalman. 1998. "Paper-and-Pencil Algorithms in a Calculator-and-Computer Age." In *The Teaching and Learning of Algorithms in School Mathematics*, edited by L. Morrow and M. Kenney, 7–20. Reston, VA: National Council of Teachers of Mathematics.

Van de Walle, John A. 2007. *Elementary and Middle School Mathematics: Teaching Developmentally.* Boston: Pearson Education.

Van de Walle, John A., and LouAnn H. Lovin. 2006. *Teaching Student-Centered Mathematics: Grades K–3*. Boston: Pearson Education.

Watanabe, Tad. 2002. "Representations in Teaching and Learning Fractions," *Teaching Children Mathematics* 8 (April): 457–63.

Wright, Robert J., Garry Stanger, Ann K. Stafford, and James Martland. 2006. *Teaching Number in the Classroom with 4–8 Year Olds*. Thousand Oaks, CA: Paul Chapman Publishing.

Zawojewski, Judith S. 2002. "Teaching Statistics: Mean, Median, and Mode." In *Putting Research into Practice in the Elementary Grades: Readings from Journals of the NCTM*, edited by Donald L. Chamberts. Reston, VA: National Council of Teachers of Mathematics.

Zawojewski, Judith, and J. Michael Shaughnessy. 2000. "Data and Chance." In *Results from the Seventh Mathematics Assessment of the National Assessment of Educational Progress*, edited by Edward A. Silver and Patricia Ann Kenny, 235–68. Reston, VA: National Council of Teachers of Mathematics.

Index

Baek, Jae-Meen, 26
Balances
    equality relationships, 57–58
    mean, median and mode, 150
Bar graphs, 143, 145–47, 153, 156–57, 163
Barrett, Julie, 162
Base-ten concepts
    counting and, 15
    decimals fractions, 47
    multiplication and, 22–23, 27–28, 33
    and nonstandard units, 125
    subtraction and, 132–35
Battista, Michael T., 82, 86
Bickel, Cindy, 76
Burns, Marilyn, 83, 130

Campbell, Patricia F., 22
Cardinal numbers, counting errors, 3–4, 6
Carle, Eric, 76, 115
Carpenter, Thomas P., 8–9
Cartesian graph paper, 105
Categorical data, graphing, 145–47
Categories of data, and data analysis, 155
Central tendency, measuring
    common errors, 148–50
    research findings, 150–51
    teaching strategies and activities, 151–52
Chapin, Suzanne H., 38, 46
Charting, for multidigit multiplication,
    27–28
Circle counting game, 5
Circle graphs, 147
Circus Shapes (Murphy), 83
Classifying. *See* Sorting and classifying
Clements, Douglas H., 82, 86, 118, 123–24
Clocks and More Clocks (Hutchins), 115
Closure discussions, assessments during, 169
Cloudy with a Chance of Meatballs (Barrett),
    162
Cockburn, A., 111
Coin values, identifying
    common errors, 116–18
    research findings, 118
    teaching strategies and activities, 118–21
"Compare: difference unknown" subtraction
    problems, 9
Complete the Clock game, 112
Concept cards, 83
Congruence, 81, 95, 97–98
Conservation, in measurement, 124
Constructed-response questions, 169

Context, meaningful. *See* Real-world
    examples
Coordinate grids, coordinate geometry
    common errors, 88–92
    research findings, 92
    teaching strategies and activities, 92–95
Copley, John V., 140
Counting
    common errors, xv, 119
    fractions, 42–43
    teaching strategies/activities, 4–6
    as pattern, 51–52
    place value and, 15–16
Critical thinking
    about addition and subtraction, 136
    about algebraic expressions, 59
    about area and perimeter, 130–31
    about decimals, 46–47
    about division, 33
    about graph coordinates, 93
    about sorting and classifying, 140–41
    about statistical concepts, 150
    during counting, 6
Cuisenaire® Rods
    equality relationships, 59
    measurement, 125
Curriculum and Evaluation Standards
    (NCTM), 165

Data analysis. *See also* Probability
    common errors, 152–54
    introducing young students to, 137
    teaching strategies and activities, 155–58
Data displays
    common errors, 142–45
    research findings, 146
    teaching strategies and activities, 146–48
Days of the Week fraction bar, 40
Decimals, adding and subtracting
    common errors, 43–45
    research findings, 46
    teaching strategies and activities, 47–48
Denominators, in fractions, 42
Developing Number Concepts Using Unifix
    Cubes (Richardson), 10
Diagnostic interviews, assessments using, 167
Digi-Blocks®
    decimals, 46, 48
    division, 33
Digits *vs.* numbers and numerals, xiii, 19,
    23, 32, 44–46

National Mathematics Advisory Panel
   goals related to fractions, 42
   goals related to pattern recognition, 49
Negative values, 95
Nonexamples, when teaching geometry, 82
Nonstandard units, 125, 129–32
Nontraditional shapes, 36
Number balances, 58–59
Number lines
   decimals, 46
   fractions, 43
   multiplication and division, 22–23
Number-logic riddles, 6
Numbers
   measurement units *vs.*, 124
   numerals and digits *vs.*, xiv
   words for, and counting, 4
Numerators, in fractions, 42

100-charts, 121
"One-one" principle of counting, 4–6
Onyefulu, Ifeonm, 83
Open-ended questioning, assessments using, 167–69
Ordering
   coins, 120
   decimals, 45–46
"Order-irrelevance" principle of counting, 4
Ordinal numbers *vs.* cardinal, 3
Origami animals and conservation of area, 129
Overgeneralization errors
   addition and subtraction, 9–10, 13
   algebra, 59
   algebraic thinking, 56
   base-ten renaming, 132–35
   counting, 3–4
   division, 29–32, 39
   examples, xiv–xv
   fractions, 37–39
   geometry, 81, 86
   multiplication, 20–21
   using measurement units, 132–34

Paper-folding for understanding reflection, 100
Parker, Andrew, 127
Partitioning, in measurement, 123
Partner work, assessments during, 166
"Part-part-whole: part unknown"
   subtraction problems, 9

Part-whole relationships
   equality relationships, 57–58
   teaching strategies and activities, 10–11
   and understanding fractions, 38
Pattern blocks
   fractions, 42
   functional relationships, 65
   geometry, 81, 86–87
   rotational symmetry, 97–98, 100
   sorting and classifying, 141
   spatial geometry, 101, 106
   tessellation, 130
Pattern recognition
   and algebraic thinking, 49, 68–70
   conceptualizing
      common errors, 50–51
      research findings, 51
      teaching strategies and activities, 51–55
   measurement units, 136
   probability, 158–61
Performance tasks, assessments using, 169
Perimeter *vs.* area
   common errors, 127–29
   research findings, 129–30
   teaching strategies and activities, 130–32
Petty, Wesley, 118
Pigs on a Blanket (Axelrod), 115
Place value
   decimals, 48
   error patterns, 13–14
   multidigit numbers, 24–25
   research findings, 14–15
   teaching strategies/activities, 6, 15–16
Prekindergarten
   addition and subtraction, 9–12
   algebraic thinking, 49
   probability, 161–62
   sorting and classifying, 137–39
   studying solid figures, 87
*Principles and Standards for School
      Mathematics*, 21–22, 146, 155
Prisms, naming errors, 84–86
Probability. *See also* Statistics
   common errors, 158–61
   research findings, 161
Problem-solving, practical, 76, 129–30

Quadrilaterals, categorization errors, 78–81

Real-world examples
   data sets, 156–57